Publish
Your Own
Novel

Connie Shelton

The following trademarks appear in this book: BizPlan Builder, Pagemaker, Quark Xpress, Corel Ventura Publisher, Pacioli 2000, Peachtree, QuickBooks, Quicken.

ISBN 0-9643161-6-1
LCCN 96-85198

First printing 1996

Although the author and publisher have exhaustively researched all sources to ensure the accuracy and completeness of the information contained in this book, we assume no responsibility for errors, inaccuracies, omissions or any other inconsistency herein. Any slights against people or organizations are unintentional. Readers should consult an attorney or accountant for specific applications to their individual publishing ventures. Listing of any organization, publication, product or service does not imply an endorsement or recommendation by the author. Readers are urged to conduct their own research as to suitability for their needs.

Attention Colleges and Universities, Corporations, and Professional Organizations: Quantity discounts are available on bulk purchases of this book for educational training purposes, fund raising, or gift giving. Special books, booklets or book excerpts can be created to fit your specific needs. For information, contact: Marketing Dept., Columbine Books, P.O. Box 456, Angel Fire, NM 87710 1-800-996-9783

To my mother, who always said,
"If you want the job done right, do it yourself."

And to my dad, who must have
passed along his entrepreneurial genes to me.

Acknowledgments:

As always, neither this book nor any of my others would have happened without the love, patience, and encouragement of my wonderful husband, Dan—you are the best.

Thanks and gratitude to my two editors, Susan Samson and Mary Cimarolli, for keeping your cool under deadline and providing much needed suggestions.

And, in the publishing world, much thanks to Marilyn and Tom Ross, who held my hand through the publication of my first book and showed me how to do everything right. And to all the writers out there who have invited me to speak to your groups, who've asked questions, and who have encouraged me in this endeavour.

Other books by Connie Shelton

Deadly Gamble: The First Charlie Parker Mystery
Vacations Can Be Murder:
     The Second Charlie Parker Mystery
Partnerships Can Kill: The Third Charlie Parker Mystery
     (forthcoming early 1997)

The above three titles are also available in unabridged audio from
Books in Motion.

Readers are encouraged to contact the author with comments and ideas for future editions of this book. Connie
Shelton is available for speeches and seminars on writing and
publishing.

Connie Shelton
Columbine Publishing Group, Inc.
P.O. Box 456
Angel Fire, NM 87710

Connie Shelton began her early life as a die-hard mystery fan. She planned to become Nancy Drew when she grew up, but life took her in many other directions. She is a commercial hot-air balloon pilot and holds the women's world altitude record for size AX-4 balloons. Her biography has been featured in *Who's Who of American Women, The World Who's Who of Women, Outstanding Young Women of America*, and *5,000 Personalities of the World*.

She is the author of the Charlie Parker mystery series and has published nine books, hardcover and soft, fiction and non-fiction. Her books have been reviewed in *Publisher's Weekly, Library Journal*, and *Booklist*, along with dozens of genre-specific publications nationwide. Her essays and short stories have won a variety of awards, and the Charlie Parker mysteries have been published in unabridged audio by Books in Motion.

Shelton is a frequent speaker at mystery conventions, writing, and publishing conferences. Contact her in care of Columbine Publishing Group to inquire about availability for your conference or classroom.

Table of Contents

Chapter 1

Why Self-Publishing?

Why would you consider publishing your own novel? If you've reached the point of picking up this book and browsing, you probably already have an idea.

Perhaps you have heard horror stories from authors who've dealt with the large New York trade publishers — cover art that did not depict the story inside, editing that sapped the flavor from the original prose, and probably the worst, books with a shelf life shorter than a carton of milk.

Possibly you've already tried the trade publishers. A stack of rejection slips may litter your desk. You don't understand why. The comments may range from "your writing is strong, I like the characters, the setting is great, but . . .(fill in the blank with one of a dozen excuses)," to "sorry, we're not accepting any submissions right now." Face it, they receive a hundred times more manuscripts than they can publish and in today's publishing world, unless yours looks like it will achieve blockbuster status, it most likely won't even get looked at.

According to a recent *Publisher's Weekly* article, more money is being spent on fewer books nowadays. This leaves a lot of writers unable to get a publisher to accept their work, while celebrities and bestselling authors get the huge advances. Even if you are accepted by a trade publisher, the road is not always easy. Far from offering editorial suggestions to help the writer along, today's editors process paper. They either want you or they don't, but they won't nurture you. We have also spoken with a number of multi-published authors who have been dropped or not renewed by their big publishers.

Times are tough.

That's why the small press movement in this country is exploding. In 1970, there were 3,000 publishers listed by the R.R. Bowker Company. By 1995, that number had increased to 42,000! Most people who think of publishers can name only the largest dozen or two New York trade houses. Obviously, small presses are becoming a major force. Some of the growth rates reported by these small presses are phenomenal. In late 1995, *Publisher's Weekly* featured the fastest-growing small presses in the country. Of the 26 companies listed, growth ranged from 8% to a whopping 370%! Industry-wide during the same period, according to the Association of American Publishers, sales rose an average of 5% across most publishing categories.

It is estimated that 400,000 people write book-length manuscripts in the U.S. each year. Roughly 50,000, or slightly over 10%, make it into print. On average, 80% of the books published are non-fiction, 20% fiction. And yet, according to the Book Industry Study Group, over 50% of books purchased are fiction. Roughly two-thirds of consumers purchase one or more adult books a year, about 44% of those are mass market paperback, 31% trade paperback, and 25% hardcover books. The average book remains in print about a year, although many stores will pull books that are not selling well within four to six months. So how do you fit into this picture?

Can you assure that your books will stay in print longer than a year? Absolutely. Can you keep them on the store shelves beyond a few short months? We'll suggest some ways. With the increasing popularity of computers and desktop publishing software, there is no reason why anyone cannot publish a book, a beautiful, first-quality book.

This book is written with that in mind—to help you step-by-step with the process of creating and marketing your own books, and to do it in a businesslike and professional manner. The term self-published has suffered some negative connotations in the past, books that are perceived as not being good enough for a "real" publisher, patched together photocopied jobs with cheap binding.

No more.

The book you are holding in your hands is self-published. The author has produced hardcover fiction titles that cannot be distinguished in any way from a bestseller trade hardcover. And you can do it, too.

Some success stories

Your motives for self-publishing may be many and varied. Perhaps you like the idea of controlling your book project, start to finish. Maybe you have been thinking about starting a home business as a means of phasing out of your current job or earning some extra money. According to a recent issue of Home Business News Report:

- The number of full and part-time home-based businesses recently hit 24.3 million.

- In a three-year study, 20% of average small businesses survived, but among home-based businesses, the survival rate was 85%!

- It is estimated that a new home-based business starts every 11 seconds, nearly 8,000 new ones each day.

- While large corporations eliminate jobs, small business creates jobs; they are the real growth generators in today's economy.

- Average home business income is over $50,000 a year, and many earn six figures.

In their book *Country Bound™ Trade Your Business Suit*

Blues for Blue Jean Dreams™ authors Marilyn and Tom Ross tell how many Americans, looking to escape the big city life, are doing so by starting their own home businesses. As self-publishers themselves, the Ross's can testify that a publishing business is one of the most ideal for a home business situation.

Two of the most notable self-publishing successes in recent years happen to be fiction. *The Celestine Prophecy* by inspirational speaker James Redfield was originally published by the author. He sold 90,000 copies himself before Warner picked it up for a mere $800,000. Marlo Morgan originally published 300 copies of her account of her Australian walkabout, *Mutant Message Down Under*. She sold them at lectures, printed more copies, and eventually sold out to Harper-Collins for $1.7 million. Both stayed on the *Publishers Weekly* bestseller lists for more than six months.

Of course, there are also numerous success stories about non-fiction titles, including *What Color is Your Parachute?* and *The One Minute Manager*. More recently, *Butter Busters, The Five Rituals of Wealth,* and *The Girls with the Grandmother Faces* were sold to large trade houses. According to a recent *PW* article on self-publishing, the major houses are now sending scouts out looking for self-published successes.

Why? Because you've done the work for them. You've made the marketing effort, you've generated word of mouth demand for your book, and now they are willing to pay big bucks.

Sounds good. But how do you get started? That's what this book is all about. Other manuals deal with non-fiction self-publishing. But none address the particular angles of selling fiction. In fact, one of the long-time gurus in the field comes right out and says don't bother with fiction. It'll never sell.

This author disputes that. I believe James Redfield and Marlo Morgan would dispute it. Having polled over thirty other fiction S-P'ers, I believe that the majority view their self-publishing ventures as rewarding in many ways, including financial.

So, this book is written with the fiction self-publisher in mind. It assumes that you are seeking commercial success, although there are certainly the other considerations we've already mentioned. As one self-publisher of four titles recently commented, "I finally took back my life!"

TIP: An advertisement that starts out "Manuscripts Wanted" usually signals that this is a vanity or subsidy press.

A word about vanity or subsidy presses

We've all seen them. Those ads in writers' magazines that begin "Manuscripts Wanted." That's your signal that this is a vanity or subsidy press.

How are they different from self-publishing? You are spending your own money to publish your book either way, aren't you? *There's a world of difference.*

Vanity and subsidy presses charge top dollar for their services. A few years ago, we ran a comparison which showed that, for a 285 page book, softcover, 2,000 copies, a subsidy press would charge $12,000. Working with a book manufacturer, the identical book bids came in at less than $8,000. And the subsidy publisher had the nerve to say that they were sharing the cost of production—the $12,000 was only *half* the cost.

The subsidy press would very generously give the author 40 copies of his own book. Additional copies could be *purchased* at a discount. This is after you've already paid to have the printing done!

So, were they going to make up the difference in publicity and promotion? No. The book would get a listing in their catalog and they would send out review copies.

Review copies from subsidy publishers get thrown in the trash. Reviewers know the names of these companies. They will not give them the time of day. Some have admitted that they don't even open the packages from subsidy and vanity presses before trashing them. *Don't* brand yourself this way!

These companies will tell you how Mark Twain, Walt Whitman, Edgar Allan Poe, and other famous authors have paid to have their work published. What they don't tell you is that these authors self-published, they did not pay vanity presses.

So, the reasons for self-publishing are many — retain creative control over your work, set your own pace with publicity to see that your books stay on the shelves longer, structure your own author tours, work from home, and **make more money**. Ready to learn more?

What to write — choosing your genre

This may not even be a valid question. Chances are, your genre has chosen you.

If you grew up devouring every Nancy Drew mystery, cut your teeth on Travis McGee, and did your internship with Kinsey Millhone, you are a lifelong mystery fan. You'll not likely turn to writing sci-fi. If your life truly exists on some other planet, if you are only happy when Star Trek comes on TV, and you speak Klingon fluently, you'll most likely not become a romance writer.

That's not to say you might not have experimented with other fiction. I wrote two family sagas before realizing that I didn't care for the format and switched back to my one true love, mystery. The two unpublished novels were great practice and doing them convinced me that I had what it takes to fill 500 sheets of paper with words. They languish on the shelf and will probably never be published. Talk to almost any successful author — most of them have some of those books.

What's the point? The very first thing you wrote might not be saleable. This could be why other publishers have turned it down. Writing is a craft, and it takes a lot of work to perfect it.

But, how do you know? You get very little feedback in this business. Seek input from others—qualified, objective people. Not your mother, not your neighbor, not your co-workers. You need valid input from someone who knows writing. Join a critique group (provided it doesn't include your four best friends), or work with an experienced editor. Critique groups can be found within many writer's organizations. Look for a group that focuses on the same kind of book you write. The group should be limited in size so that all members get a chance to have their work critiqued. Preferably, it should be a group with a mix of experience among the members—some new to writing, some with experience. If you cannot find a critique group in your area, how about checking with a creative writing teacher at the nearest school?

Editors and "Book Doctors" are becoming increasingly available. See the Appendix for some suggestions. One hint: find someone who specializes in fiction, in your genre if possible. Send them a few sample pages or a couple of chapters before committing to have them do your entire book. Look at the suggestions they make. Feel comfortable that the two of you are on the same wave-length.

Be sure they will do a full line edit and critique. In addition to structure and plot flaws, you need someone who will catch typos, missing words, etc. By the time you've written and typeset your book, you are too close to it to be objective—in fact, any manuscript becomes too familiar after you've read it twice. Don't try to edit your own book. The few little mistakes you miss will brand the book as unprofessional.

TIP: Always have someone else proofread your book, after all other editing is done.

One more word about genre vs. mainstream fiction. The word "mainstream" has become a watered-down catch-all for books that can't seem to be categorized. While this may seem like a good idea because it seems that a mainstream book will appeal to everyone, not just genre fans, it actually works against you. The big publishers avoid the terminology and so should you.

Why? Because bookstores and libraries also have a hard time with mainstream, not knowing where to shelve the books or which customers to recommend them to. The closer you can come to defining your book in terms of genre, the easier time you'll have.

Remember, most genre have sub-genre. In mystery, there's the hard-boiled PI, the police-procedural, the cozy, the historical, and so on. Romance has the gothic, the romantic-suspense, the sensual. Even westerns are classified as historical or modern. If your book comes close to the borderline with any of these, it will reach a more distinct readership than a "mainstream" book.

If you simply cannot classify your book within a genre, look for a catchy angle. One small Colorado press has had good sales with a historical mainstream book. The angle involved a timely topic (spouse abuse) and how the main character handled her situation during a time in history when such things were not discussed openly. The author does lots of radio interviews and speaking engagements where she discusses the timely angle of the story. Her book has gone into a second printing.

If you are relying solely on bookstore personnel or librarians to present this timely angle to your audience, it may or may not come across. Again, you can make your point in a genre book as well, and you have a better chance of getting it into the stores and into the hands of your audience.

TIP: Writers groups are one of your best networking opportunities.

Another reason to choose genre fiction: networking with other writers. Every genre has its support group:

Western Writers of America
Romance Writers of America
Mystery Writers of America
Sisters in Crime (brothers are welcome, too)
Sci-Fi, Fantasy Writers of America
Society of Children's Book Writers
Christian Writers Guild
International Association of Crime Writers

See the Appendix for addresses. If you do not belong to one or more of these groups, check into it *now*. They offer tremendous support to members and a wealth of marketing ideas particular to your field.

One caution: some writers groups discriminate against self-publishers (the old prejudice that self-published books are not as well written). Best to approach them slowly. See if you can join as an unpublished writer. You'll still get their newsletter and marketing ideas. Even without published author status, you are getting most of what you want from the organization.

I've found that individual members are usually very friendly and not the least bit denigrating about your being self-published. In fact, many of them are curious about how you did it and thrilled by your successes. They'll ask questions and you can point them to this book as a guide to getting started.

Do you have what it takes?

You're thinking about starting a publishing business. Assuming that you want to publish commercially successful books, you need to view starting your publishing business just as seriously as you would look at starting any other business. First, take the short evaluation test below. Be honest with yourself. Do you have the money to commit to a business venture? If not, can you get it? Can you perform the daily duties required, such as writing your own advertising copy, handling your finances, dealing with customers? What talent resources do you have? Which will you need to hire out? You may have never run a business before, but that's not as important as your attitude toward the venture.

Think, too, about your motivation and publishing goals. Do you plan to publish one book and work to drive it to super-stardom? Do you plan to build a career gradually for yourself with multiple books? Or maybe to take on other authors and expand your publishing company into a mid-size or large house? You don't need all the answers at this point, but formulating goals and having a vision is important.

We talk about commercial success, but this is not to say that you can't publish other types of books—more personal topics such as family histories or genealogies, poetry, personal essays. See Chapter 12 for a section on those types of books.

SELF-PUBLISHING ASSESSMENT WORKSHEET
Check the answer that best describes you or your feelings.

Independence:
___ 1. I want to be my own boss. I am highly motivated and a self-starter.
___ 2. I'm fairly independent, but I don't want to make all the decisions by myself.
___ 3. I am not a self-starter. I would rather have the security of letting someone else worry about the problems.

Entrepreneurial spirit:

___ 1. I like controlling the direction of my projects.

___ 2. I want to give input, but would like someone else to help with the decisions.

___ 3. I do not want too much responsibility. I'd rather someone else handled it all.

Financial status:

___ 1. I have money I can afford to risk in a business of my own.

___ 2. I have great ideas but not much money. I could do it with some outside investors.

___ 3. I want to be assured of payment for my writing.

Business knowledge:

___ 1. I have some experience in business or management.

___ 2. I have a general understanding of business, but I could use some help.

___ 3. I have no business experience and can't even balance my checkbook.

Ability to "toot your own horn."

___ 1. I have written a good book, and I want the world to know about it.

___ 2. Although I am normally shy, I know that books need promotion to sell so I will do it.

___ 3. I have a hard time promoting my own work.

Time to promote your book:

___ 1. I realize that writing a book is only the first step. I know I will also need to invest time and money in promotion.

___ 2. I'll spend time on promotion, but I don't want the full responsibility or time demands.

___ 3. I would prefer to write the book, then turn it over to someone else.

Public appearances:

___ 1. I am comfortable speaking in front of audiences when I feel I have something important to say.

___ 2. I need more confidence with public appearances but am willing to learn.

___ 3. Even the idea of signing books in a store makes me queasy.

Selling skills:

___ 1. I enjoy the satisfaction of selling a product I believe in.

___ 2. I don't like direct sales but can promote a product through mail order, advertising, or via wholesalers.

___ 3. Writing is an art. I don't feel that it is proper to openly solicit sales.

Now tally your score. Record the number of answers you have in each category below.

___ #1 answers

___ #2 answers

___ #3 answers

Review your answers. If you checked mostly number ones, you would probably be happier self-publishing than having a large publisher handle your books. If you checked mostly number twos with some number ones, you can still make a go of self-publishing with some outside help. If you checked mostly number threes, you should definitely go the traditional publishing route. (If you checked #3 on the last two questions, you might rethink whether you want to write for publication at all. Even a trade-published book is going to require some publicity effort on the author's part.)

Remember, you can hire or barter for some of the duties involved. For instance, as previously mentioned, you should not attempt editing your own book. You can hire a book doctor or editor, or perhaps work a trade (your computer time for their editing time, etc). Work a similar trade for accounting and tax preparation, or perhaps get a part-timer in to help you with filling orders or stuffing envelopes. Most of these things can be worked out. The main thing to evaluate at this point is your attitude toward starting a business and toward marketing your books once in print.

Also, talk to some published authors, those who have sold to the big trade publishers. The successful ones will tell you that they put a great deal of their own time and most of their advance money into promotion. They generally don't show a profit until they have several books out. On the other hand, we showed a profit on our very first title, within 90 days of its publication date.

So, if you're going to write the book anyway and you're going to do most of the promotion yourself, why not handle the middle steps of working with the book printer and cover designer, filing your own ISBN and copyright forms, and shipping the books out to bookstores, libraries and wholesalers? Of course, it's not quite that simplistic, but it's close. And you have the freedom to work at your pace to keep those books on the store shelves.

Speaking of profit, have you ever wondered who gets what from the sale of your book? This survey came from the *L.A. Times* in 1994. Figures are based on the average book price of $23.50 by a trade publisher.

Bookseller	$11.28 (48%) **
Publisher	$ 4.93 (21%)
Production Cost	$ 3.06 (13%)
Author	$ 2.00 (9%)
Promotion	$ 1.88 (8%)
Agent	$ 0.35 (1%)

**[We assume this includes the wholesaler's cut]

It's easy to see that, as an author who sells to a trade publisher, you are near the bottom of this totem pole. By also taking for yourself the publisher's portion and the agent's portion, you are suddenly looking at making 31% on the sales of your book, after production and promotion costs.

Now, *that* picture looks a little more pleasant.

Chapter 2

Starting Your Business

Start with a plan

Developing a business plan can be a tedious, time-consuming headache. It can also be extremely enlightening. It can also be a *requirement* if you are seeking financing for your project.

No matter how well you believe you have thought out your business venture, doing a business plan is sure to bring up some questions that you have not considered. If nothing else, the exercise will lead you to *think*. And isn't it only smart, before investing your money or someone else's in a new business, to consider all the angles?

Look for fill-in-the-blank forms at your office supply. There is also software out today, such as BizPlan Builder from JIAN Tools for Sales, Inc., that will walk you step-by-step through the process. Some are so comprehensive that they seem like overkill for a small one-book publisher, but we suggest that you go through it anyway. If nothing else, filling in the blanks and gathering the data will test your dedication to your business venture. And you will have a *whole* lot clearer picture of the time and money required to start your business.

If you seek financing for your new business, the business plan will show your banker or other potential investors that you are serious and professional in your approach. Bankers are often reluctant to make loans to new businesses, so every bit of preliminary research in the form of a formal business plan will be a mark in your favor.

Part of doing your business plan will be to outline your marketing approach. Don't breeze through this part, believing that it will take care of itself. It won't.

TIP: Tackle the easiest parts of your business plan first, those things you already know. Then go back through it and fill in the missing data.

In fiction selling, you need to reach all three levels of customer — the reader, the bookstore, and the wholesaler or distributor (more on those in Chapter 7). You might have little trouble getting a wholesaler to carry your books, but if the bookstores aren't ordering them and the readers aren't buying them from the stores, you'll end up nowhere.

So, your first task will be to figure out who and where your readers are. What will be the least expensive way to reach them? Marketing approaches are covered in depth in Chapter 6, but you need to be thinking about this three-level approach very early in your planning.

We suggest that you read this entire book before you begin writing your plan. Take notes or highlight areas of interest. If you've never owned or managed a business before, you might want to read some general business books, too. See the Appendix or visit the business section of your local bookstore for additional help.

Step by Step - Starting your Business

Financing your venture

Ways of coming up with capital to start your business abound, if you just look for them. Here are some that other publishers have used.

Probably the easiest source of money, if you have it, is your own. This might come from savings, rental income, stock dividend income, an inheritance, your retirement fund or severance package from a previous job. If your own resources are sufficient, this will be the quickest and easiest way for you to obtain money.

If you have some money, but not quite enough, you might approach your banker for an unsecured personal loan. Ask for it before you need it. For instance, if you have a $10,000 savings account, but estimate that you'll need $15,000, you'll have much better luck getting that $5,000 loan if you already have money in the bank. If you spend your $10,000 first and then ask for $5,000, good luck. If you have a good rapport with your bank, and a good credit rating, you might be able to get a signature loan on your personal guarantee.

Another possibility might be to take out a home equity loan, borrowing against the value you've built up in your home. This money can usually be used for any purpose, and the interest rate you'll pay is normally considerably lower than some other sources.

Do you have a life insurance policy that has accrued some cash value over the years? Check out the possibility of borrowing against it.

Use your credit cards. If you have a good credit record and have always paid your balances off on time, you can probably request and get a higher credit limit on some of your cards. We know one self-publisher who financed most of her business expenses for the first two years this way. Just keep in mind that credit card interest rates are usually higher than with most other forms of borrowing.

How about friends and family? Parents can make gifts of up to $10,000 a year to each of their children, free of gift tax. If both Mom and Dad contribute, this can be up to $20,000. If a gift isn't possible, how about a loan? Approach three or four people who might each be able to lend part of the total.

Pre-sell books. Mail flyers to your entire personal mailing list announcing your forthcoming book. Solicit pre-publication orders on a prepaid basis. Give them an expected delivery date. This approach probably won't yield more than a few hundred dollars, but it's worth doing.

How about bartering? You may be able to cut production costs by bartering some of the services you need. If you might otherwise have to pay for typesetting, you may find someone willing to trade their time for an item or a service that you could provide. Cover design, printing of stationery and forms, legal services, tax preparation, or warehouse space are some things you might not have to lay out cash for if you can work a trade. (Remember bartered items are taxable from an IRS standpoint.) Most larger firms will not be able to do this, but if you are working with another one-man business, this might be an alternative.

Venture capital clubs exist for the sole purpose of investing in new businesses. Call 203-323-3143 to order the *Directory of Venture Capital Clubs*. This is where doing a well-thought-out business plan will pay off. When you make your presentation to the investors, you need to appear professional and well-educated as to your knowledge of the business, and demonstrate a dynamic marketing plan.

The government also offers many programs that can help new businesses get a start. Contact the Small Business Administration at 800-827-5722 to locate the SBA office nearest you. Also check the library for the book, *Government Giveaways for Entrepreneurs* by Matthew Lesko.

Choosing a company name

Your company name will be with you for a long time. Research it carefully. Decide whether you want your company name to reflect the types of books you publish or to remain more general, giving you the freedom to branch into other areas.

The name Intrigue Press has worked very well for our mystery, suspense, adventure line, but when we decided to publish non-fiction titles, it wasn't quite so appropriate. We incorporated under Columbine Publishing Group, Inc. and turned Intrigue Press into a subsidiary of that company. It might have been simpler to choose a more generic name from the start.

On the other hand, our distinctive spider web logo and the words *Intrigue Press, Publishers of Mystery, Suspense, and Adventure*, might just be responsible for the quick response our titles get from bookstores. The envelope probably sparked more interest than a generic name like XYZ Publishers. In direct mail, if they don't open the envelope, it doesn't matter what you're advertising inside.

Another factor that makes me believe in the distinctive name theory has been our experience with a co-op mailing. Lumped together with three other publishers in a generic envelope, a recent mailing to 2,000 bookstores didn't pull nearly as well as our own mailing to only 800 stores. The flyers inside the envelopes were the same.

Naming your company is your decision. You should include a descriptive word like "publishing," "press," or "books" in the name. Romance, Inc. has a whole different connotation than Romance Publishing. Think it over carefully, come up with three or four or a dozen ideas, and run them past other people. After you've narrowed down the list, you'll need to do some research.

In some states, it is illegal to use the same name as another business, particularly if you are incorporating. Your state corporation department can tell you if the name you want is in use.

Whether or not you can legally use the name you have chosen, it just isn't smart to use an existing name or one that is very similar to an existing publisher—especially if the other company has been around a long time. It would be a common assumption for anyone learning about your title to send their order to the older, more established company. At best, this could lead to confusion, with the order eventually finding its way to you. At worst, it will be lost forever and you'll have a mad customer somewhere out there.

Why not just use your own name?

As mentioned earlier, there are still some prejudices against self-published books. If your company is called Smith Publishing, the editor-in-chief is Sandy Smith, and the lead title this season is by Sandra Smith . . . well you get the picture. You'll be readily recognized as a self-publisher.

In some states you are required to file a fictitious name statement if your company uses any name other than your personal one. This is usually done on a simple form with sometimes a small fee and running a notice in the newspaper. Check with your own state to find out what its requirements are. The business guides, *Starting and Operating a Business in [State]* are available for all 50 states and give lots of good information on the specific regulations in your state as well as the generalities of starting a business anywhere.

Check sources such as *Literary Market Place* (available at your library), *Writer's Market,* the publishers section of *Books in Print*, and the *Small Press Record of Books in Print* for availability of the name you have chosen. There are now computer CDs with listings from the yellow pages of the entire nation. This is an excellent way to find out whether a business name exists anywhere in the country.

TIP: Consult your accountant or attorney to help choose the form of business best suited to your situation.

Deciding on a form of business

All businesses are formed in one of four ways: either as a sole proprietorship, a partnership, a Limited Liability Company (sometimes called a Limited Liability Partnership), or a corporation. There are a few variations on these, but basically those are the choices.

A sole proprietorship is the easiest to form and the simplest from a tax standpoint. It also offers the least protection of your personal assets. You use your Social Security number as your business tax ID number, and file Schedule C with your regular tax form 1040. Of course, you still need to keep good business records to justify your tax deductions, and it's easiest to do this if you keep a separate business bank account rather than co-mingling your personal and business money.

A partnership is formed by any two or more persons or entities who wish to go into business together. The partner can be your spouse, a friend, an investor, or someone whose business sense you trust. It is said that partnerships are like marriages, easy to get into and expensive to get out of.

If you want to go this route, know your partner(s) well, and get everything in writing. You can get fill-in-the-blank partnership agreements at office supply stores or you can have an attorney draw one up. The main thing is to reach agreement with your partners as to how you want the business structured, and to have that agreement in writing.

The tax requirements of a partnership are a little more complicated than those of a sole proprietorship. The partnership is an entity in itself and must file its own tax return. The resulting profit or loss is passed on to the partners in whatever percentage each owns. The partners then declare the profit or loss as personal income on their own tax returns.

Be aware that each partner is responsible for all debts of the partnership, regardless of which partner incurred the debt. Be careful.

A corporation provides the most personal protection, something that might be desirable if there is the potential of litigation in your business activities. Your corporation, even if owned by one stockholder (yourself), is a legally separate entity with no connection to your personal assets. Although in today's litigious society, where anyone can sue for anything, there are no guarantees.

The procedure for forming a corporation varies from state to state. You do not have to be incorporated in the state where you reside, so if your state's procedure is complicated or expensive you can do it elsewhere.

In New Mexico, it is a matter of filling out a two page form, called Articles of Incorporation, and sending it to the State Corporation Commission with a check for $100. Approval comes in two to three weeks if you mail it in, about an hour if you walk the paperwork through personally. To stay legal, you need to hold annual meetings of your Board of Directors, adopt a set of by-laws, and file a bi-annual report with the state.

Delaware is another state known for easy and inexpensive filing of corporate forms.

Tax wise, a corporation is treated as a separate entity, and files its own tax return. A regular corporation pays corporate income tax, then any earnings paid to the shareholders are taxed again as personal income to the individual. To avoid this double taxation, there is an election that small business owners can take. This is called the S-Corporation election. Certain criteria apply as to the size of the business and number of shareholders. If you meet these (and most home businesses will), you can file a form with the IRS to make this election. They will determine whether you will be allowed S-Corp status.

The main benefit of S-Corp status is that, although the corporation files a tax return, it does not pay tax. Instead, the income is passed through to the shareholders and taxed only once, on the shareholder's return. Check with your own state's Corporation Commission or Department and with the IRS for the regulations that apply.

Another form of business entity, which is relatively new, is being recognized by almost all states now. It is called, depending upon where you live, a Limited Liability Company (LLC) or Limited Liability Partnership (LLP). This form of business affords the liability protection of a corporation, with a structure and accounting procedures more like a partnership. Forming an LLC or LLP is similar to forming a corporation, in that it is usually regulated by your state's Corporation Department. Since these are relatively new forms of business, check with your own attorney or state regulatory agency to find out the specific rules.

There are several good books available on the subject of starting a business and choosing its form (see Appendix).

Each person's situation varies, and we advise that you read more on the subject and check with your own tax consultant before making any decision.

Your business address

Unless you have unlimited funds, or have access to a rent-free office space, you'll probably start your business in your home. Again, check your local zoning ordinances to find out if a home business is legal. In most places, as long as you don't have extra cars parked in front of the house all day, generate extra traffic in the neighborhood, or put up signs out front, you should be okay.

A small publishing business doesn't usually require any regular employees, especially at first, and you don't need a sign on the property. A daily stop by the UPS truck shouldn't be considered extra traffic.

TIP: Think carefully about the address and phone number you'll use before having cards and stationery printed.

Although you operate from home, there are reasons you might want to use a post office box for your business address instead of your street number.

If you sell a lot of books in your own city, people may recognize that your publishing company address (which will be printed on the copyright page of every book) is in a residential area. If you generate many fans (we should all be so lucky) you may get people showing up at your door. Some of the attention may not be wanted and some can be downright harmful. In this day of stalkers and nut-cases, one cannot be too careful.

The old perception that a business using a post office box is somehow more likely to flee into the night has changed. Key people like your banker and your book printer will still have the street address. But every person nationwide who reads your books doesn't need it. So, get a post office box.

The reason that this is a consideration so early in the game is that you will need an address for everything you do from this point on. You'll have it printed on your stationery and your checks. It will appear on the title page of your books. You'll use it when you register your business with the state and federal government. Do it now.

Open a checking account in the business name. Even if you've decided on a sole proprietorship as your form of business, it's better not to mingle funds. You will only have a clear picture of how your business is doing if you can't easily write checks out of that account for groceries and bills. Plus, it is much more professional when working with your vendors to use business checks.

Being legal

You'll need to obtain state and federal tax numbers.

Every state that collects sales tax will have a department that handles it, usually in the state capital, probably called the Taxation and Revenue Department or something similar. Call them to find out what you need to do. Our state has a one-page form to fill out and no fee. You receive your own tax ID number and a packet that explains what percentage you need to collect on your in-state sales and how to go about filing the required reports. You don't collect or pay tax on out-of-state sales or sales to anyone who will be reselling the product (like bookstores). Again, this may vary from one state to the next, so check with yours.

If you chose sole proprietorship as your form of business, you'll use your Social Security number for your Federal taxes, so nothing further is required until tax time. If you formed a partnership, LLC, or corporation, your business needs a separate federal tax ID number. It's called a Federal Employer Identification Number or FEIN, and you get it from the IRS. Call them to get form SS-4. The form calls for basic information and the IRS has a procedure whereby you can telephone them once you have the form filled out and receive your number almost immediately.

Once you hire your first employee, life becomes tremendously more complicated. You'll be liable for Social Security withholding, Medicare withholding, unemployment taxes, and possibly workers' compensation insurance. There are quarterly reports to file to report these taxes. If you incorporated, remember, the corporation is a separate entity and you become an employee of your own corporation. Any salary you pay yourself becomes subject to all of the above.

You can go a long way before you need employees. All your editing, cover design, and book printing can be contracted on a book-by-book basis. Even temporary help with envelope stuffing and office chores can be done by your own family members or by temporary helpers without necessarily putting them on the payroll. It can get complicated. This is why we suggest consulting your own tax pro before making these decisions.

Setting up the office

Presumably, as a writer, you already have a work space and computer that you've been using. As we mentioned, a spare bedroom or basement can be converted into a wonderful home office. Even a corner of another room will suffice for awhile.

You've chosen your business name and perhaps thought about a logo. Now you can get your business stationery and cards printed. Shop around, as prices vary widely. The Appendix at the back of this book lists some inexpensive mail order sources for printing and office supplies. Most will send you paper samples so you'll know what you're getting ahead of time.

Compare. If you live in a big city, you may have access to inexpensive print shops. Those of us in small rural places have to shop a little more carefully.

What else do you need in the way of equipment?

A computer and laser printer are a must. If you don't already have them, consider them the best investment you'll make. Currently, computers can easily be bought for $2,000 or less; laser printers are under $1,000. You'll do your own typesetting on your laser printer — 300 dpi models work fine, 600 dpi is better. If you compare the cost of typesetting a 200 page book vs. buying the laser, you'll realize that the first job pays for the new printer.

What about software?

There are page layout programs that make typesetting your book pages a breeze. Pagemaker, Quark Xpress, and

Corel's Ventura Publisher are good choices. If you don't already have one of those and don't want to put out the money just yet, most word processing programs will work quite well. You need to be able to produce headers and footers and have consecutive page numbering. You'll want some flexibility with fonts. If your program will do these, you can set up your page layouts easily enough.

An accounting program that allows you to track inventory and do order entry is also important. You'll be selling to other businesses, bookstores and wholesalers. They expect to receive an invoice with each shipment and a statement at the end of each month.

Interactive billing, receivables, payables and inventory control will simplify your life. There are publisher-specific programs on the market ranging in price from $800 to $8,000. A one-author publisher certainly doesn't need anything that complex. If you decide some day to take on other authors and would need to produce royalty statements and reserves against returns, you can always upgrade.

We use an accounting program called Pacioli 2000 that retails for $49, with a street price of around $28. Its eight modules are completely interactive, so when you bill an order to your customer, the charge is automatically posted to accounts receivable and the items sold are deducted from inventory. Some accounting experience is helpful when using Pacioli for the first time. It doesn't have cute little icons, or checks that look like checks, but it's as comprehensive as some accounting packages that we've seen costing thousands.

QuickBooks by the developers of Quicken, or Peachtree are other business programs worth looking into. If you aren't at all good with numbers, you might want a simple order entry program for your daily billing and have your CPA do the financial statements for you.

If everything pertaining to billing and inventory control is beyond your realm, there are numerous fulfillment houses, including some book printers, who will bill and ship your orders. There is, of course, a fee for this service. The Appendix lists some fulfillment services.

A copier is nearly a must. Although you can run to the copy shop, it becomes tiresome, inconvenient and expensive very quickly. We design all our own flyers and advertising pieces on the computer and run copies on our home office copier. It is a Canon model that cost about $800 six years ago. It has probably paid for itself several times.

Look for a copier that enlarges and reduces the image size. A feeder, which automatically sends the originals onto the copy tray one sheet at a time, and a collator are nice features but are usually found on more expensive models. Shop around to figure out what your budget can manage.

Faxes and Phones

Much of the world today operates over the fax machine. If you don't have fax capabilities built into your computer, get a machine. A separate fax machine has some advantages over the computer kind. If you have artwork that you've cut and pasted together, rather than generating it on the computer, you'll need the separate machine to fax it to anyone. Or if you have to fill out a form (such as for the government) or sign a bid and return it (such as for your book printer), it's easier with a separate machine. If your funds are limited, you can get by without one for awhile, but do put it at the top of your wish list.

A discussion of fax machines brings up the question of whether you should have a separate phone line for the fax or use your regular line and a fax/phone switcher box. Our experience with the switcher boxes has been that they don't work very well. After trying three different brands, we opted for a separate line. Perhaps improvements have come along since.

And speaking of phone lines. Should you have a separate line for your business or use your home number? You can do either, but you should decide as early as possible. After all, you're going to have all those business cards and stationery printed. Use a number you can live with at least until you're ready to reprint your stationery.

We feel a separate business phone line is a plus.

1. You won't have to check the time when the phone rings to see if you're still on business hours, and decide whether to answer with the business greeting or just "Hello."

2. You can instruct your children never to answer the business phone—less confusing than letting them answer the home phone sometimes, but never between eight and five. Children younger than teens should never answer a business phone.

3. You can record a professional sounding message for the business line apart from the "Hi, Dick and Jane aren't home right now," that may be on your home line.

4. If you live on the West Coast, it's better to let your business answering machine catch that East Coast caller than to pick up with a sleepy "Hello" at six a.m.

Your choice, but the time to decide is now, before you have much printing done.

And, speaking of phones, this might also be the time to consider having an 800 or 888 toll-free number. If you plan to let customers order directly, this is nearly a must. You pay for the call, which is free to the caller. Costs have come down dramatically in recent years. You can get a toll-free number that rings on your regular line, so you don't have to pay for a separate line. Most have low or no-monthly fees. And the per-minute charges have come down, from the 60-70¢ a minute rates of several years ago, to as low as 13¢ a minute with some carriers.

Another customer amenity is the ability to take credit card orders. It doesn't make sense to offer a toll-free ordering number if you can't immediately take the order. And you don't want to get into the hassle of having to hold a phone order and wait for the check to arrive. So, you really do need to be a credit card merchant before you activate your toll-free service.

Merchant status is arranged through your bank. Contact the customer service department. Some banks are easier to work with than others on this. If you live in a big city and don't have a personal banking contact, you may have some difficulty. Many card companies don't want to work with start-up businesses. Most of them are leery about mail order. In our small town, we had no trouble. Of course, we've been long-time customers of this bank and have several accounts there. All you can do is ask.

If your bank refuses to work with you on this, all is not lost. Publishers Marketing Association and SPAN (addresses in the Appendix) are publishing organizations that you'll want to join anyway for the great networking opportunities and marketing ideas. As a member, you can obtain merchant credit card status with very favorable terms. There is still an application process, but at least they are small publisher-friendly. Check with SPAN or PMA for the details.

Becoming a credit card merchant is not something that you must do right at the start, either. You may want to see what direction your business takes and decide whether this service would be a benefit to your customers.

Storage

The other "must" is a clean, dry place to store your books when they arrive. A garage is fine or a rented storage locker. Be sure the roof doesn't leak. A basement isn't usually a good choice because you are going to have to unload 100 or more cartons of heavy books when the freight company delivers them and carry them down a flight of stairs. Then, as you ship them out, you'll be carrying them back up. Better to have a place on ground level. If a truck can back up to it, that's perfect.

You'll need boxes sized to contain various quantities of books, and sealing tape and mailing labels. Our books arrive from the printer in cartons of 30-40 books each, depending upon the thickness of each title. So, for orders of 20 books or more, we simply ship them in those same cartons. We order shipping boxes in two or three other sizes to handle smaller orders. For single copy orders and review copies, we get flexible corrugated cardboard like the book clubs use. Being tacky on one side, it seals shut in seconds. Stick a label on the outside and it's ready to go. See the Appendix for the names of companies that sell shipping supplies.

Your mailroom should also have a work table for packaging and a mailing scale.

You can load your packages into the car every day and drive them to the post office or UPS office and stand in line, but that tends to get old real fast. We enjoy the convenience of having our own shipper number with a daily pickup by the UPS driver. It's easy to do.

Call your local UPS office and tell them you want to establish a shipper account. If you live in a large city, an account rep will probably call on you and explain it all. In our case, being in a small rural town, they simply sent the start-up packet with our driver. He took a few minutes to explain the various forms and procedures.

You will be issued your own shipper book, with your company name and shipper number imprinted on it, along with a supply of tracking labels and a rubber stamp with your shipper number. As you seal each carton you're shipping, stamp your shipper number on the box, weigh it, and write an entry in the shipper book. Make arrangements with your driver as to where he/she will pick up the packages each day. In our case, we have a screened porch, protected from the weather. This is an ideal place because the driver doesn't have to ring the bell and we don't have to be home when he comes. You can work out whatever arrangement is good for you.

This daily service (5 days a week) costs only $8.00 per week. It's well worth $1.60 a day not to carry those boxes across town to the UPS office, especially on the days when we ship five or six 40-pound cartons.

Anything else?

A couple of other start-up expenses will easily earn their costs back in the long run.

Subscribe to *Publishers Weekly*. Call 800-278-2991 to order. Yes, it's expensive as magazines go, but you need to know what's going on in the publishing world. Most of the talk is about New York publishers and big name authors, and at first glance, you'll wonder what pertains to us little guys. But at least scan it cover to cover each week. We have found sources for display products, freelance editors, possible sources for subsidiary rights to our titles (audio and mass market paperback), plus some innovative marketing ideas (usually in the Bookselling Daybook section).

Plus, *PW* runs a call for information each week, asking publishers to submit material pertinent to an upcoming issue. This appears in a little box at the bottom of the table of contents page. They run special issues each year featuring mystery, romance, religious titles, sci-fi, children's and others. When they call for information on your genre, send them a press kit on your newest titles and any timely information on what your company is doing. They sometimes run these little tidbits, even coming from small presses.

Join SPAN and Publishers Marketing Association. The addresses are in the Appendix of this book. Both do co-op advertising and offer chances to display your titles at major trade shows such as ABA, ALA and Frankfurt. The SPAN newsletter carries a regular column on fiction publishing.

One last tip: whether you decide to self-publish or not, if you get nothing else out of this book, follow this tip. Start a "Publicity Ideas" file right now. Gather every scrap of publicity and marketing information you get your hands on and keep it here. With a good supply of up-to-date genre information and marketing ideas, you'll never be faced with the helpless feeling that you can't think of a single way to sell your books.

What does it cost?

We're often asked how much it costs to start a publishing business and print the first title. Not to dodge the question, but it varies quite a bit with each situation. When we started, we already had computer and software, a laser printer and a copier. We've added other equipment over the years, but the big stuff was already in place. We budgeted $20,000 to cover our business setup expenses, the first print run of 3,000 books, mailing supplies and stationery, and to do the publicity for the first title. Add another $3,000 to $5,000 if you are starting without any equipment at all.

As to the cost of printing the books, again, this will vary. All factors, such as trim size, paper weight and color, format (hard or soft), page count, and quantity must be factored in. In general, our production costs are usually somewhere around $10,000 to $12,000 for a print run of 3,000 books, including cover art and freight. Our least expensive book to date was a hardcover with full-color jacket at $2.78 per book. Our most expensive was a softcover anthology, two-color cover, 156 pages at over $4.00 per book (because it was a very small print run).

Doing business professionally

Remember, you are doing business with other businesses now, and you want to appear as professional as possible.

People will perceive your company as large, small, or microscopic based on the image you present to them. Don't give yourself a bad image.

Accounting practices

If you just can't cope with learning a computer accounting program right now with everything else you're doing, you can keep a manual ledger of your accounts. Get some invoice and monthly statement forms from the office supply, have them preprinted at the same place that prints your stationery, or make them on your laser printer. Keep a separate ledger page for each customer and write each invoice into your account ledger on the correct customer's page. Post each payment as it comes in. Go through your ledger pages at the first of each month and type up a statement of account for each, showing all open invoices. Mail the statements promptly.

Some customers will not pay from the first invoice they receive. They require a statement of account to match the invoices against, so they know exactly where they stand with you. Pay attention to each customer's billing requirements. Letting receivables fall behind has been the downfall of many businesses. Stay on top of it. Know who owes you money and call them before they get behind.

Keep track of your tax deductible expenses, such as office supplies, phone bills, travel expense, etc. Virtually every cent your business spends should be deductible. The key is in keeping good records. If you use a computer accounting program, you'll enter each expense into a category as you write the check. If you are on a manual system, at least make a note in your check register of each expense category. Your bookkeeper or accountant can then transfer the totals to your profit and loss statements.

Setting terms and conditions for your customers

There are some aspects of selling in the publishing business that are different from that of other wholesale/retail industries. Trying to buck the system will not make the old pros change their ways, it will only make you look like an amateur. Learn how they do it and adapt.

One standard practice in publishing that you don't find in other industries is the matter of returns. If the bookseller or wholesaler is unable to sell your books, they can return them to you — and you are expected to issue credit for the returned books.

This practice started many years ago, as the publisher's way to get booksellers to try a wider variety of titles, and to be willing to take books from unknown authors. Today, returns might not seem like a very fair business practice — after all, shouldn't they take as much risk on a book as you are taking? Yet, the alternative is that they don't buy your books at all. That's the bad news.

The good news is that you can set some reasonable restrictions on returns. Books should be in saleable condition when you get them back. Returns must be made within a reasonable period of time. Standard time limits range from a few months to a year or more. Set whatever is comfortable for you.

Other terms you should decide include discount schedules, payment terms, shipping costs, whether you require prepayment on new accounts, whether you accept credit card orders, etc. A copy of our Terms and Conditions is shown on the next page.

You may notice that we have two different discount schedules—with and without return privileges. If an order is sold on a non-returnable basis (with the higher discount), we use a red-ink rubber stamp to indicate on the invoice that the books are not returnable because they were specially discounted. So far, most of our customers settle for the lesser

Intrigue Press

Publishers of Mystery, Suspense, Adventure

Order Acceptance:
1. All orders are binding upon Intrigue Press only after acceptance by us.
2. All new accounts are required to prepay orders until credit is established.
3. Accounts wishing to establish credit are required to complete and submit an account application.
4. Special handling requests must be received with the order.
5. Customer agrees to abide by all terms and conditions herewith.

Pricing:
The standard Discount Schedule (with return privileges) is as follows:

1-2 books	no discount
3-4 books	20%
5-99 books	40%
100-up	50%
(in even case lots)	

A special Discount Schedule is offered on titles sold on a non-returnable basis.

10-99 books	50%
100-up	60%
(in even case lots)	

Other special discounts or payment terms are not available. Prices subject to change without notice. Prices slightly higher outside the U.S.

Shipping:
1. All titles in stock are shipped within 24 hours. For titles not in stock (i.e. pre-publication) we will supply customer with an estimated shipping date.
2. FREE shipping on prepaid orders. FREE shipping on orders of 10 copies or more shipped to one address.

Payment terms (on accounts with credit approval):
1. 2% 10, Net 30. Discount forfeited after 90 days.
2. 2% per month interest charged after 30 days.

Returns:
Unblemished books may be returned for credit or refund if received within 6 months of the original invoice date. A copy of the original invoice must accompany the return shipment. Shipments must be returned postage-paid to: Intrigue Press, 21 Mammoth Mtn Rd, Angel Fire, NM 87710. Unblemished books are not torn, mutilated, scuffed or defaced in any way. Books purchased under the special discount schedule above are not eligible for return.

Ordering:
Intrigue Press provides three methods for direct ordering:
1. Phone 1-800-996-9783. MC & Visa accepted on new accounts.
2. Fax your order to 1-505-377-3526 with credit card info for new accounts.
3. Mail orders (with payment enclosed on new accounts) to: Intrigue Press, P.O. Box 456, Angel Fire, NM 87710.

Welcome to Intrigue Press. We look forward to doing business with you!

Example of Terms & Conditions

discount with the return option.

Bookstores expect to receive a 40% discount on their purchases. This is what they get when they order through a wholesaler. However, you are not expected to sell them a single copy, or even two or three, at that large a discount.

Our discount schedule, with return option, is:

1-2 books	No discount
3-4 books	20%
5-99 books	40%
100-up	50% (in even case lots)

We found some resistance to ordering five books when we were a one-book publisher. Many stores would rather start with only 2 or 3 copies of a title. In that case, we suggested that they order through Baker & Taylor or Ingram (more on getting set up with a wholesaler in Chapter 7). Now that we offer more titles, stores don't mind ordering one of this and two of that, to get to the 40% discount range. You can set your discount breaks where you wish, but you won't make much profit if you ship one book, discount it 40%, and have to wait 30-60 days for your money.

One caution: You may be tempted to make exceptions to your terms and conditions at times. Don't do it. Once you have established your terms, they are, in effect, carved in stone. The Federal Trade Commission has regulations prohibiting businesses from offering different terms to like customers. You may offer different terms to your wholesale accounts vs. retail customers, and you may offer different terms to libraries than to stores. But with *like* customers, between one bookstore and the next for instance, you must give them all the same terms. Several major trade publishers were sued by the American Booksellers Association, accused of this very thing—giving more favorable terms to the chain stores over the smaller independents.

Now that your business is formed, you can begin the steps toward publishing your first book.

Chapter 3
Early Activities

There are a few more "paperwork" things you need to do to start the process of publishing that first title. Send for the information suggested here. The companies listed below will provide specific instructions at the time you request their packets. Review everything carefully. Not following the rules could eliminate your book from some important listings.

TIP: Remember, your book printer is not your babysitter. It's your job to apply for and get your ISBNs, EAN symbols, and listings in important publications. Do your homework.

ISBN

The International Standard Book Numbering system has been adopted so widely that a book will find an almost impossible time getting into the commercial market without its own ISBN.

ISBNs are assigned to each publisher and your unique publisher prefix will always be yours. You will be assigned a block of either ten, one hundred, or one thousand numbers. Write to the R.R. Bowker Company at 121 Chanlon Rd., New Providence, NJ 07974 or call 908-665-6770 for the application. You'll need to do a little pre-planning here. If you never plan to publish more than your own one or two books, a block of ten will be sufficient. If, however, you think you might take on some other authors and your list could conceivably grow beyond ten titles, you should go ahead and apply for a block of one hundred. There is a fee of $115.00 when you apply for your publisher block of numbers, regardless of how many numbers you get.

All ISBNs are ten digits long. The differences in the blocks of numbers are defined by where the dashes are placed and they look something like this.

Blocks of ten will resemble: 0-1234567-8-9
Blocks of 100 will resemble: 0-123456-78-9
Blocks of 1000 will resemble: 0-12345-678-9

Your publisher prefix is the second group of numbers, the ones after the zero. The last two groups of numbers are the ones unique to each book. Obviously, the smallest publishing houses will have single digits in the last two number segments. The larger houses will have larger blocks of numbers after their prefix.

There are some small publishers who will swear that these single digit ISBNs will brand a book and unfairly prejudice reviewers and bookstores against you. As a publisher who is stuck with one of these single digit ISBN blocks (having not the faintest idea in the beginning that we would ever publish more than two books), we don't believe this assertion is true. Every title we've submitted, so far, has been reviewed in at least one of the major review sources and *all* have been carried in bookstores nationwide. The probable reasons for this are discussed in detail in Chapter 5.

So, your decision, when applying for your ISBN block, should be based on how many books you think you will publish.

INTERNATIONAL STANDARD BOOK NUMBERING. UNITED STATES AGENCY.

International Standard Numbering System for Books, Software, Mixed Media etc.
In Publishing, Distribution and Library Practices
121 Chanlon Rd., New Providence, New Jersey 07974 908-665-6770

International Standard ISO 2108

R.R. Bowker • A Reed Reference Publishing Company   (FAX) 908-665-2895

APPLICATION FOR AN ISBN PUBLISHER PREFIX

FOR AGENCY USE ONLY
SYMBOL: _____
PREFIX: _____

PLEASE PRINT OR TYPE:

Company Name: _____

Address: _____

_____

Phone Number: _____ Fax Number: _____

Toll Free Number: _____ Telex Number: _____

If P.O. Box Indicated, Local Street Address is Required:

_____

Name of Chief Operating Officer: _____

Title: _____ Phone Number: _____

Name of ISBN Coordinator/Contact: _____

Title: _____ Phone Number: _____

Division or Subsidiary of: _____

Imprints: _____

PAYMENT -
A ONE TIME SERVICE CHARGE OF $115. FOR PRIORITY SERVICE SEE REVERSE SIDE

_____ Check/Money Order enclosed. Make payable to "R.R. Bowker "

_____ Charge: _____ American Express _____ Visa _____ Master Card

     Account #: _____ Expiration Date: _____

Total amount enclosed or charged: $ _____

Our company hereby applies to the ISBN U.S. Agency for an ISBN Publisher Prefix.

Authorized signature: _____

Title: _____ Date: _____

(Continued)

Director: Emery I Koltay • Officers: Peter Simon, Carol Cooper, Albert Simonds, Donald Riseborough, Lynn DeVita

ISBN Application

Bookland EAN Scanning Symbol

Another marking that has been adopted throughout the industry is the Bookland EAN Scanning Symbol or barcode that you will find on the back cover of nearly every commercial book nowadays. Wholesalers and booksellers are increasingly reluctant to accept books that do not carry the EAN symbol.

It's easy and inexpensive to obtain them. We call our supplier, place the order over the phone, and receive the symbol on film the next day (via either Federal Express or Airborne), ready for the printer. It only costs around $25 per title, so do it. See the Appendix for suppliers of Bookland EAN scanning symbols.

Library of Congress Catalog Number

The LCCN is a number that is pre-assigned to a book. The key word here is pre-assigned. You cannot get an LCCN for a book that is already published and there are certain rules about which books qualify. Write to the Library of Congress, Cataloging in Publication Division, 101 Independence Ave. SE, Washington, DC 20540-4320, and request the PCN Publishers Manual. It contains the rules and an application form. Send the completed application in early (about the time you begin typesetting the book). Part of the requirement for obtaining an LCCN is that you furnish the Library of Congress with a copy of your finished book after it is printed.

Copyright Form TX

Literary works are registered with the Copyright Office on form TX. Write to them at Register of Copyrights, Library of Congress, Washington, DC 20559-6000 and request Form TX and the instructions for it. To file your copyright, you need to complete this form and send it back along with a check for $20 and two copies of your finished book.

REQUEST FOR PREASSIGNMENT OF LIBRARY OF CONGRESS CATALOG CARD NUMBER

NOTE: *Card numbers cannot be preassigned to books which are already published. Works that receive a preassigned Library of Congress catalog card number are not eligible to receive Cataloging in Publication data for that same edition of the work.*

FORM MUST BE TYPED

DATE: __4/18/95__

PUBLISHER'S NAME ON TITLE PAGE: __Intrigue Press__

YOUR NAME: __Lee Ellison__

PHONE NUMBER: __505-377-3474__

Type the complete address to which the preassigned card number should be sent. (This will be your return mailing label.)

Intrigue Press
PO Box 456
Angel Fire, NM 87710

FOR CIP OFFICE USE

Library of Congress Catalog
Card Number preassigned is:

95-077210

Transcribe the information in items 1-8 exactly in the form and order in which it will appear on the title or copyright pages of the printed book. Use only those abbreviations which will actually appear on these pages. (**Please attach a copy of the proposed title page, if available.**)

1. Author(s) __Connie Shelton__

2. Editor(s) __Leslie Lenz__

3. Title __Vacations Can Be Murder__

4. Subtitle __The Second Charlie Parker Mystery__

5. Edition (exactly as printed in the publication, e.g. second edition, revised edition, etc.)____

6. U.S. place of publication: City __Angel Fire__ State __New Mexico__

7. Any copublisher(s) and place __none__

8. Series title and numbering, exactly as printed in the publication ____

9. Approximate number of pages __216__ 10. Number of volumes ____

11. ISBN (Hard cover) __0-9643161-1-0__ ISBN (Paperback)____

12. Proposed date of publication: Month __Jan__ Year __96__ 13. Language of text, if other than English ____

14. Does (or will) the title in item 3 appear at periodic intervals, e.g. annually, quarterly, etc.? ☐ Yes ☒ No

For each title which is preassigned a Library of Congress catalog card number, the Library of Congress requires one non-returnable complimentary copy of the best edition of the published book. If selected for the Library's collections, the book will be cataloged. This copy is in addition to copyright deposit copies. Continuing participation in the PCN program is contingent on full compliance with this obligation.

Send this form to: Library of Congress
Cataloging in Publication Division
101 Independence Ave., S.E.
Washington, DC 20540-4320

Searching notes:

FOR CIP OFFICE USE ONLY.

RECD: ____
ASGN: ____
SENT: __DATED APR 2 0 1995__
APIF: ____

607-7 (rev 6 /94)

Completed LCCN form

CERTIFICATE OF REGISTRATION

FORM TX
For a Literary Work
UNITED STATES COPYRIGHT OFFICE

This Certificate issued under the seal of the Copyright Office in accordance with title 17, United States Code, attests that registration has been made for the work identified below. The information on this certificate has been made a part of the Copyright Office records.

TX 4-125-504

EFFECTIVE DATE OF REGISTRATION

Marybeth Peters

10 13 95

OFFICIAL SEAL

REGISTER OF COPYRIGHTS
United States of America

DO NOT WRITE ABOVE THIS LINE. IF YOU NEED MORE SPACE, USE A SEPARATE CONTINUATION SHEET.

1 TITLE OF THIS WORK ▼

Vacations Can Be Murder: The Second Charlie Parker Mystery

PREVIOUS OR ALTERNATIVE TITLES ▼

PUBLICATION AS A CONTRIBUTION

2 NAME OF AUTHOR ▼
a Connie Shelton

DATES OF BIRTH AND DEATH
Year Born 1951

AUTHOR'S NATIONALITY OR DOMICILE
OR Citizen of USA

NATURE OF AUTHORSHIP   full text

3 YEAR IN WHICH CREATION OF THIS WORK WAS COMPLETED 1995
b DATE AND NATION OF FIRST PUBLICATION   Month 10 Day 1 Year 95

4 COPYRIGHT CLAIMANT(S)
Connie Shelton
PO Box 416
Angel Fire, NM 87710

APPLICATION RECEIVED OCT. 13 1995
ONE DEPOSIT RECEIVED
TWO DEPOSITS RECEIVED OCT. 13 1995
FUNDS RECEIVED

MORE ON BACK ▶

Copyright Form TX

For now, request the forms and have them on hand. See the publishing checklist in the last chapter of this book to remind you to file the form after your books have arrived.

Books in Print

To get your titles listed in the all-time bible of book titles, *Books in Print*, is a simple matter. Along with your ISBN application, you should have received Advance Book Information (ABI) forms from the Bowker company. Complete one for each new book, as far in advance as possible, preferably as soon as you have decided on a publication date (more on that in a minute). Your book will be listed in *Forthcoming Books in Print* as well as *Books in Print*. There is no charge.

Once *Forthcoming Books* has received your ABI form, you will be contacted about running an annotated (paid) listing in this publication. We did this for our first title and honestly cannot say whether we received more orders as a result. Go to your library and browse through *Books in Print*. You'll see the annotated listings and can decide for yourself whether your book might be typical of the listings you see. If not, don't spend your money.

Small Press Record of Books in Print

Dustbooks publishes the *International Directory of Little Magazines and Small Presses*, the *Directory of Poetry Publishers, Directory of Small Magazine/Press Editors and Publicists, Small Press Record of Books in Print*, and *Small Press Review*. Write to them at: Dustbooks, PO Box 100, Paradise, CA 95967-9999. Request their listing forms to have your titles listed in the appropriate publications. Also send finished books to *Small Press Review* for review in this monthly magazine.

ADVANCE BOOK INFORMATION

R. R. BOWKER DATA COLLECTION CENTER
P.O. BOX 2068, OLDSMAR, FL 34677-0037

TITLE: Vacations Can Be Murder

SUBTITLE: The Second Charlie Parker Mystery

SERIES: Charlie Parker mysteries

Foreign Language: Translation ☐, from what language:

AUTHOR(S): Connie Shelton

EDITOR(S): Leslie Lenz

TRANSLATOR(S):

ILLUSTRATOR(S):

INTRO. BY; PREFACE BY; etc.

ILLUSTRATIONS YES ☐ NO ☒

PAGES: 216

AUDIENCE(Select Primary Audience):

College Text☐   Young Adult ☐: Grade:

Elhi Text ☐: Grade: Juvenile ☐: Grade:

x General
Original Paperback ☐

Revised ☐   Abridged ☐   2nd Ed. ☐   Other:

PUBLICATION DATE: July 1995
Reprint ☐: If reprint, name of orig. publisher & orig. pub. date:

ISBN NOTE: Put full 10 digit number with hyphens in spaces below.
The system requires a separate ISBN for each edition.

ENTER PRICE(S) BELOW: INT'L STANDARD BOOK NUMBER
On short discount (20% or less) ☐

HARDCOVER TRADE: 21_95   ISBN _0_-_9643161_=_1_-0_

If juv., is binding guaranteed?

PUBLISHER(Not Printer): Intrigue Press
Address   21 Mammoth Mtn Rd.
               P.O. Box 456
               Angel Fire, NM 87710

Telephone (505) 377-3474
    fax   (505) 377-3526

DISTRIBUTOR, if other than publisher:
(If you distribute foreign books you must be their exclusive U.S.
distributor. Please send us a copy of your documentation
for exclusivity)

IMPRINT (if other than company name):

THIS WORK IS ESSENTIALLY (Check one)

☒ FICTION (mystery)   ☐ TEXTBOOK

☐ POETRY   ☐ BIOGRAPHY

☐ DRAMA   ☐ OTHER _____
                                      Specify
☐ CHILDREN'S FICTION

☐ ESSAYS

PRIMARY SUBJECT OF BOOK
(Be as specific as possible)

☐ MEDICAL (MB)   ☐ SCIENCE/TECHNICAL
                              (ST)
☐ CHILDREN (CB)

☐ LAW (LB)

☒ OTHER (Specify):
   Mystery
   Detective
   Adventure
   Women's fiction
   Hawaii locale

LIBRARY BINDING: _ _._ _	ISBN _ _ _ _ _ _ _ _ _ _	
HARDCOVER TEXT: _ _._ _	ISBN _ _ _ _ _ _ _ _ _ _	
PAPER TRADE: _ _._ _	ISBN _ _._ _ _ _ _ _ _ _ _	
PAPER TEXT: _ _._ _	ISBN _ _ _ _ _ _ _ _ _ _	
TCHRS. ED.: _ _._ _	ISBN _ _ _ _ _ _ _ _ _ _	
WKBK: _ _._ _	ISBN _ _ _ _ _ _ _ _ _ _	
LAB MANUAL: _ _._ _	ISBN _ _ _ _ _ _ _ _ _ _	
OTHER: SPECIFY _ _._ _	ISBN _ _ _ _ _ _ _ _ _ _	

LC#

Order # (optional):

Completed by *Lee Ellison*

Completed ABI form

Choosing Your Publication Date

Choosing your pub date will be one of the most important choices you make and you need to determine it early, while you are filling out those ABI and LCCN forms. It would seem that once you've written the book and sent it to the printer, you would consider it published as soon as those finished books hit your doorstep. You can do it that way, but don't.

Many events hinge upon your pub date, some of which we'll go into in detail later. For now, estimate when you will send the book to press and when the finished books will be in your hands. Choose a pub date about two to four months *after* your finished books are due from the printer.

Is there such a thing as an ideal time of year to launch a new book? Probably not, but here are some hints that might help you decide. In trade publishing, the "seasons" are spring, summer, and fall. Most large publishers make a big push, launching new titles in spring (April, May) and again in the fall (September, October). Summer novels (June and July) are usually the ones thought of as "beach books" or a good read while on vacation. If you publish your book in any of these months, you will be competing with a lot of other titles for review space.

August has typically been considered a dead month in mail order businesses. People are cramming in the last of their vacation time and getting their kids back to school. November and December are not good months to solicit new orders from retailers (like bookstores). They ordered their holiday stock during the fall months, and are now working their tails off doing all the business they can during the holiday rush. They don't want to talk about placing new orders.

This leaves January, February, and March as the seemingly ideal months for a small press book to get extra attention. Any of these would probably be a good choice for getting that coveted review space. In our own experience, we've had books reviewed during these slower times, but we've also had them reviewed in the peak months of April and October. Each publisher should examine his or her own situation. If your schedule works out so that your choices might be December or January, take January. August or September, take September. Otherwise, go with a month that fits well into your timetable.

We'll discuss getting reviews in more depth in Chapter 5.

TIP: Contact authors early to solicit blurbs. Six months before sending the book to press is not too soon.

Getting Blurbs or a Foreword

Having a flattering quote from a well-known author in your genre can go a long way in selling your books. Start early to obtain them.

If you've followed our advice and joined writer's organizations within your genre, hopefully you've met some of the "names" in your field. Obviously, the ones you've become friends with would be the easiest to approach. If you don't have that advantage, go through the membership list of said organization and choose several of the biggest names. (I'm a firm believer in starting at the top.)

From the membership list, you should be able to get mega-author's home address or personal post office box address. This would be quicker than writing to them in care of their publisher, but that can be an option, too. Write to several of them, asking most respectfully if they might find the time to read your book and provide a comment. Meanwhile, make a "B" list of your second choices for possible endorsements.

Don't be terribly disappointed if people like Stephen King refuse your request. They get thousands of demands on their time. If you are lucky enough to have a mega-author agree to a blurb, send your manuscript off to them as quickly as possible, including enough postage to cover the return manuscript. If none of the heavy-hitters respond, go to your second list. Sooner or later, you'll get someone to agree.

Be sure to write a thank-you note to your endorsers, and send them a finished copy of your book.

What if you're so friendly and well known among your fellow writers that you could easily get twenty or thirty blurbs? Use a little caution here. Some booksellers, as well as critics, have the feeling that we authors stick together a little too much. Some feel that one author will make up great quotes about another author's book without having actually read it. (Well, it's been known to happen.) The more general the blurb, the more likely they are to believe that the blurber never read the book. You can request that your blurbs say something specific. Rather than a "Welcome to the genre" comment, something like "Joe Author's Billy Character is gutsy, smart, and not above causing a little trouble," is better. You might suggest a comment or setting—you know your book; ask for what will be helpful.

If your book, although fiction, contains material of a technical or scientific nature, or something else that required a lot of research on your part, you might look for an expert in that field to write a foreword. Although a foreword is more commonly found in a non-fiction book, it can be done in fiction as well, lending greater credibility to the research.

Establish Your Mailing Lists

Another early activity you can work on while your book is at the printer is establishing your mailing lists. Obviously, before you've gone this far, you should have done your business plan and you know who your likely customers are: bookstores, libraries, romance readers, mystery fans, etc.

We'll go more into the specific ways to reach these readers

in chapters 6-9 on marketing, but you should start now gathering names. We have been in mail order businesses for over 20 years, and our pet axiom is "never throw away a name."

Put them all in your database. Start with friends, family, neighbors, business associates — every name you can think of. Add to this the members of organizations you belong to (provided they don't forbid the use of their membership list for mailings). Some writer's organizations offer their members mailing lists of bookstores, libraries, and reviewers that are friendly toward the genre. Take advantage of these sources by purchasing the lists and adding them to your database as well.

One caution about mailing lists. Commercial mailing list companies do not normally sell their lists. The fee you pay is for a one-time use of the list. You may not use the names again without renting it again. The renter seeds the lists with names that will clue them if you use it more than once. Of course, once you have made a sale or generated a sales inquiry from your mailing, those leads may be added to your own list.

You can compile your own mailing lists in many ways, by researching at the library. Gale Research publishes directories of every conceivable nature. They even publish the *Directory of Directories*. There are directories of media contacts, libraries, and nearly every type of business. See listings in the Appendix. This research can be time consuming, though, and renting mailing lists is always an option.

In addition, there are companies and publisher organizations that specialize in doing co-op mailings to bookstores and libraries for small publishers. Your flyer will be one of several in the envelope, but these types of mailings are very cost effective. You can find names of those who do co-op mailings in the Appendix.

Choosing your book title

You probably think this was done long ago. No doubt you had a working title for the book as you wrote it. Still, it will pay to do a little research. Although book titles cannot be copyrighted, much confusion can result when two books (especially if they fall into the same genre) carry the same title. It would seem that the odds of having chosen the exact title as someone else would be slim, but we've had it happen to us three times (out of six books). In each case, there was already a book in print with our chosen title, and we chose another.

The longer your title is, the better your chance of it being unique. A one or two-word title, especially if it is a catchy well-known phrase, is likely already out there somewhere. If you can come up with a four- or five-word title, it's not nearly as likely that someone else used that same combination of words.

Check both *Books in Print* and *Forthcoming Books in Print* to find out if the title is in use. Another excellent place to search for book titles is online at the Amazon.com bookstore. They list almost 1.1 million titles. Access them at http://www.amazon.com (also check our Appendix under Internet sites to find out how to list your own titles here). Look for other titles that are very close to yours as well. Try to make your title as different from others as possible.

Having your author photo taken

It's become customary to have a photo of the author on nearly all books, either on the jacket of a hardcover or inside a paperback. One of the reasons for this is that it's a great marketing tool. People relate much more effectively to someone when they can put a face with the name. They form a picture in their minds about what type of person you are.

The photo can be color or black and white, large or small,

on the inside or outside cover of the book. The pose can be as formal or as casual as you like. (This is fun when you get to make the decisions, isn't it?)

TIP: Let your author photo reflect the tone of your book.

You might want to look at some other published books in your genre and see what others have done. It's okay to be different, but you don't want to be so different that you come across as either too casual or boringly stiff.

In mysteries, most author photos lean toward the casual or even the thematic. Authors have been photographed holding a gun, or with a wide-brimmed hat pulled low over the eye, with their cats, or even in costume. Many romance writers use a soft-filtered, fluffy-haired glamour look. Any of these poses would be entirely inappropriate if this same person authored a business book. On the other hand, a dark suit, white shirt and tie against a solid background that would be entirely appropriate for the business book would be much too stuffy for the mystery author.

Feel free to do something fun. After all, it's your book.

One word of caution: be sure you have the right to use the photo. If you have portraits done by a professional photographer, they usually own the copyright to all the photos they take. Be sure to explain your intended use for the photo. Get permission, *in writing*, to use the photos for publicity and press kits as well as for the book cover. Some will be agreeable to this, others will not. They may want to charge an outrageous fee for unlimited use. Many portrait studios keep negatives for a specified period of time, then destroy them. Ask if you can buy your negatives and get written permission to use them in any manner you wish.

A home-done photo can work just as well, especially if you have opted for the casual look. For my second Charlie Parker mystery, which is set in Hawaii, I used a photo my husband had taken of me wearing a beautiful ginger lei. The lei had been a birthday gift from friends when we lived in the islands a couple of years before the book came out. The picture and that time in our lives are special to me, and it seemed fitting to have this wonderful reminder captured on a book in this setting.

One of our other authors, Alex Matthews, was photographed with her calico cat. It just happens that a fictional calico cat is one of the main characters in her books. The photo was taken by Alex's husband, and is a cute pose, with the author and cat practically touching noses.

Now the paperwork is done, and we're ready to get on to the fun part!

Chapter 4

Design and Production

You may be surprised to learn that you can actually do much of this phase yourself. You've composed your book and typed and edited the manuscript on your computer. Basically, what's needed is to set your words into the correct page size and type face, or font.

Trim Sizes

The finished size of a book is known as the *trim size*. Common sizes are 8-1/2" x 11", 6" x 9", 5-1/2" x 8-1/2". There are obviously many other options available, but the closer you can stay to a standard size, the lower you can keep your costs.

Hardcover or Soft?

Most commercial books are published in one of three basic formats: hardcover (with or without dust jacket), trade paperback, and mass market paperback.

Hardcover, or cloth as it is sometimes referred to, is exactly what you think: hardbound books, usually with dust jackets.

Trade paperbacks are the larger-size, soft bound (called perfect bound) books you usually see for how-to's, self-help, and other non-fiction titles. Occasionally, fiction is published in this format, as with some of Barbara Kingsolver's titles and the recent *Snow Falling on Cedars* by David Guterson.

Mass market paperbacks are the small, rack-size books you find in grocery stores, airports, and discount stores, as well as traditional bookstores.

Take a look at where your book will fit into the market. Look at the other books published within your genre or subject area. While many non-fiction books are found in the full 8-1/2" x 11" size, not much fiction is published this way. *Most* novels will be in either hardcover in 6" x 9" or 5-1/2" x 8-1/2", or mass market paperback. Since the printing and distribution angles are entirely different for mass market books, we will primarily deal with the trade paperback and hardcover formats.

The decision on whether to publish in hardcover or softcover is yours. The costs for printing either format are about the same. However, as mentioned in Chapter 1 on choosing your genre, there are some considerations other than cost when choosing your format.

TIP: Start an Ideas file. Collect copies of book covers and advertising pieces that appeal to you.

Now, do some research. Go to the biggest bookstore you can find. Go to the section where your type of books are found — mystery, romance, sci-fi, western, children's, Christian, or the closest genre to your book's subject. At a glance, you should be able to tell whether most of the titles are hardcover, trade paperback, or mass market paperback. If most of the books are mass market, what is the second preferred format? Hardcover or trade paperback?

For instance, in mystery, there are hardcovers and there are mass market paperbacks. You'll find almost no trade paperbacks. In romance, there are a few trade paperbacks, but not many. Now in children's and YA novels, there are few hardcovers (other than in the picture book category). The point is, find out what is considered normal in your genre.

Booksellers and readers alike tend to stay with the familiar.

This is a good time to analyze your book to see if it fits within publishing norms. Divide your number of manuscript pages by 1.25 to find out roughly how many finished pages you will have. Is your book significantly longer or shorter than *most* of the books in the genre? While it is rare to find any novel shorter than 200 finished pages (anything less is often considered a novella) or longer than 1,000 pages, you'll find that most genre tend to have "norms." For instance, mysteries are not normally long, long books. Tension and pacing are difficult to maintain over 400 pages. And most mystery plots need to be solved in somewhere between a few days and a few weeks of chronological story time. Westerns or romances, though, can be rich, rambling tales that span years. And family sagas will span generations. Naturally, it takes more words to develop this type of story.

From a publishing viewpoint, you need to make sure your book fits into the market for which it is intended. A five hundred page hardcover mystery that will, by necessity, be priced at something over $25, will have a hard time competing (both in size and price) with those 250-pagers at $19.95. Although pricing is certainly not the major consideration, for most book buyers it is certainly a factor. We'll cover more on pricing your book in a minute. For now, flip through a few books in your local bookstore to see how yours compares.

Layout

Now that your research has indicated which format you should use, you can get started with the layout. Find a book in the size and format you plan to use. You probably have one on your own shelf.

Measure the widths of all margins — left, right, top and bottom. The margin will be slightly wider on the bound edge of the pages. Therefore, on right hand (recto) pages, the left margin will be wider. On left hand (verso) pages, the right margin will be wider.

In your computer program, set the margins to match the measurements you've taken. If your program does not have the capability of specifying different margins for left and right pages, find a happy medium. Just be sure that your text won't be so close to the edge that it will get caught up in the binding.

Now, about typesetting. In the old days, all type was cast into tiny lead blocks and each letter was individually set into place to form words, sentences . . . an entire book. An extremely time consuming and expensive process. Now, in the computer age, we have hundreds of fonts, or typefaces, available with a couple of keystrokes. Our laser printers can produce very fine camera-ready artwork. Wherever we refer to typesetting here, we are talking about copy produced on a computer and laser printer.

If you haven't yet made it into the computer age and don't want to start learning now, you can still pay to have your pages typeset. The cost will depend upon the format you submit to the company doing the layout. Manuscripts submitted on computer disk in a word processing format will be much less expensive to typeset than typed manuscripts. Something hand written will be the most expensive.

Assuming you plan to typeset the book yourself, here are the steps. Look through the available typefaces on your computer program. Find one that is easy to read and experiment with the font sizing and spacing between lines until you approximate the layout of the example book. Notice how the headers and page numbers are done. You can experiment with a little dressier font here, but a simple one works just as well. Avoid using more than two fonts on a page, especially in a novel, which is primarily text.

For ideas on book design, browse through some of the bestsellers you have on your shelves. Big publishers pay big bucks for book design, but you can achieve many of the same effects with your own computer and laser printer.

Print out two or three sample pages to be sure you are happy with the look. Play around with different effects and print again. Work out the details using a small sampling before you import the entire text file. Specify that you wish to print *crop marks*, the marks that will tell the printer where to trim to make your 8-1/2" x 11" pages the smaller 6" x 9" trim size you want (now you know why they call it that).

Save your layout as a style file for ease in using it again and again.

Before importing the text from your word processing program, you might want to spell check one final time — word processors usually do this function better than layout programs. Use the Search & Replace feature to change double spaces to single spaces at the end of sentences. Upon transfer from the word processing program, the layout program will usually convert inch marks (") to true quotation marks (" "), double dashes to em dashes (—), and other typographical corrections. If you are doing the layout in a word processing program, check the operating manual. There are usually formatting codes or character sets that allow you to accomplish these typesetting functions.

Once you've transferred the entire text file into the proper layout (it may need to be split into small sections to accomplish this), print out the full book. Now it starts to feel real, doesn't it? These printed pages are your galleys.

You'll need to check the galleys carefully. Somehow gremlins usually manage to sneak in. Look for things like missing or improperly placed headers, footers, and page numbers. Too many spaces between words and extra blank lines that may not have been noticeable on a double spaced manuscript will jump out at you now. It would also be a good idea to have someone who has never read the book (not you or the person who helped edit it) to read through the galleys. This is the last chance to catch missing words, incorrect punctuation, etc.

Consult a style book, such as the *Chicago Manual of Style*, to be sure you've handled typographical conventions correctly.

Cover Art

You can't judge a book by its cover, right? It might not be fair, but in fact, that's exactly what happens every day.

Studies have shown that the average book buyer follows a very specific pattern. 1. Picks up book based on interesting front cover design or because of a review they've seen. (Remember, most books are shelved spine facing out, not front facing out, so that narrow strip of print is your first sales tool.) 2. Glances at front cover for approximately 8 seconds. 3. Turns book over and looks at back cover for 15 seconds. 4. *If still interested*, they will usually open the book and read the flap copy (on a hardcover) or read in detail the descriptive information on the back of a paperback. 5. Only a very small percentage ever read a word of the inside text, and most of those only read a couple of paragraphs.

Still think you can't afford to pay a cover artist? You can't afford not to.

TIP: Your cover art is your most important sales tool.

Unless you have graphic design experience, don't attempt doing your own cover art. Being "artistically inclined" isn't good enough. We're not denigrating your art talent or that of your friends, it's just that we've seen too many books die an extremely early death because the cover looks homemade. It won't get reviewed, it won't get into bookstores (very many anyway), and no matter how good the book is inside, not many readers will pick it up to find out.

So, how to find a cover designer? We've listed a few in the Appendix. Or check *Literary Market Place*. Talk to your book printer — they usually know of design firms they've worked with in the past. Tell them what type of book you are doing and ask them to recommend someone with experience doing your kind of covers. Talk to the artist. Describe what you have in mind and ask some questions about their experience in this field. Ask for a general price range. Have them send you some examples of previous book covers they've done. Many will refer you to someone else if they can't provide what you need.

Does this mean you can't have a say about your own book cover? Absolutely not! After all, this is one of the reasons you chose to self-publish — you wanted to retain control over the important stuff.

I've yet to meet an author who didn't have some idea of what he/she wanted his/her book to look like. After working for months on the story, creating the characters, setting the scene, of course you are the most intimately familiar with the book.

Before you rush off to order the design work, though, a little more research is in order. Go back to that bookstore, or your own bookshelf if you have an extensive collection of books in your genre. Pull a dozen or so books from the shelf and line them up.

What do the covers have in common? Do all the romances feature a hunky bare-chested guy? Do some of the classier ones show a single rose or a string of pearls? Do all the mysteries have a bloody dagger? Do some of them feature an intricate little scene of the murder, with possibly some hidden clues? Do the sci-fi titles show aliens and spaceships?

Well, you get the idea.

Now, look at other details. The lettering — is the title larger than the author's name, or the other way around? Are there blurbs from well known authors on the cover? Where is the author's photo located? How large is it? Color or black and white? Read the publisher hype, those few paragraphs that are meant to whet the reader's appetite. Notice the kinds of vivid words they use, the interesting ways in which they describe the book. Get a feel for it, since you will be writing the cover text for your own book.

Decide which look appeals to you most. Keep in mind that your book cover should look enough like others in the genre to be easily identified as such.

Why not be different? Well, if your sci-fi novel features a cover with a bare-chested man clutching a long-haired woman, the chances are good it will get shelved in the stores with the romances. It will never get looked at by those readers you want to reach.

You can make your cover different, but not *too* different.

If you plan to publish a series of books with the same characters, try to plan ahead with your first cover. Think of ways in which you can make all of your book covers similar enough that readers will recognize them as a series.

TIP: Don't go to your local print shop for book printing. You want a book manufacturer.

Working with Book Printers

Sometime early in the process, perhaps even before you've completely typeset your book, you'll need to get some bids on the cost of having it printed.

Where to turn?

You want to work with a book printer, not a general printer. While a regular printing house can handle the text pages, book printers are the experts at stitching, binding, covers and dust jackets. And because they have the specialized equipment to handle all these tasks in one location, they will be less expensive.

You can find a listing of selected book printers in the Appendix, or look in *Literary Market Place*.

Name _____ Phone No. _____

Company _____ Fax No. _____

Address _____ Book Title _____

City / State / Zip _____ My Account Executive is: _____

I need a print & bind quote prepared for these specifications:
(Please fill in the appropriate box and/or circle.)

1. Please quote a quantity of _____ ,
_____ , _____ , ❑ Add'l thousands

2. The trim size of my book is:
❑ 5.5" x 8.5"   ❑ 6" x 9"
❑ 7" x 10"   ❑ 8.5" x 11"
❑ Other _____

3. My page count is _____

4. Text copy to be provided as:
❑ Camera Ready Copy
❑ Digital Files ○ Mac ○ Dos/Windows

5. There are _____ **pictures**
(halftones) to print in the text.

6. The ink color in which the text will
print is:
❑ Black throughout

❑ Other _____
Proofs ❑ Yes ❑ No

7. The paper stock for my text is:
❑ 50#   ❑ 60#   ❑ 70#
❑ Uncoated   ❑ Gloss   ❑ Matte
❑ Other _____

The color of the text paper stock is:
❑ white ❑ natural

8. I will provide cover/dust jacket as:
❑ Camera Ready Copy
❑ Composite film w/color proof
❑ Digital Files ○ Mac ○ Dos/Windows

Color(s) for cover/dust jacket are:
❑ 4-Color Process (CMYK)
❑ Black + # _____ PMS colors

Do the inside covers print?
❑ No   ❑ Yes, # _____ colors
Proofs ❑ Laminated Color Proof
         ❑ Colorkey
         ❑ Bluelines

9. The cover & binding style I prefer
is:
Soft covers
❑ Perfect bound   ❑ Sew wrap
❑ Notch bind   ❑ Spiral wire

❑ Other _____

Cover stock to use:
❑ 10 pt. coated one side (C1S)
❑ 12 pt. coated one side (C1S)
❑ Other _____

Use the following cover finish:
❑ Film lamination ❑ Gloss ❑ Matte
❑ DuroSheen (UV coating)
❑ DuroMatte (UV coating)

Hard covers
❑ Adhesive case
❑ Smyth case   ❑ Notch case

Cloth to use for case:

Stamping; Foil color _____
❑ Front ❑ Spine ❑ Back

Dust Jacket paper stock:
❑ 80# Enamel   ❑ Other _____

Use the following dust jacket finish:
❑ Film lamination
❑ DuroSheen (UV coating)
❑ DuroMatte (UV coating)

10. Shrink wrap the books?
❑ No   ❑ Yes   ○ individually or
                  ___ books/package

Ship my books to: City/State/Zip
_____
_____

Be certain to provide your fax number for a quick response.

Additional comments and/or instructions: _____
_____
_____

If your specifications are more detailed, or if you have questions, please call 800–999–BOOK.

Sample book quotation form

You should plan to get bids from at least five or six different companies. Type up a request for quotation form, listing the specifications for your book. Fax or mail it to several firms and wait for the bids to come in.

One of the prime criteria that you must furnish before getting bids is how many pages the finished book will be. How can you know this before you've typeset the pages? You'll need to prepare what's known as a *castoff*. This is a best-guess estimate of the page count. It will be close enough for comparative bids.

Assuming that your manuscript was initially prepared with standard one-inch margins all around, double spaced, in 12 point Courier, take the total number of manuscript pages and divide by 1.25 to get the number of finished text pages.

Now add the number of pages for front matter. This consists of the title page, copyright page, dedication and/or acknowledgments the author wishes to include, and perhaps a listing of other titles by this author if he/she has other published works.

Most non-fiction books will also have back matter, consisting of an index, bibliography, appendices or other reference material. Usually fiction does not contain these elements, but the very back of the book is an excellent place to include an order form for all your titles. If you plan to have any back matter, add the number of pages to your castoff. Remember, the front and back of a page count as two pages.

If you want every chapter to start on a right hand (recto) page, you can estimate that approximately half of them will not naturally fall that way, and you will have to insert blank pages to make it happen.

A typical castoff might look like this:

300 Manuscript pages divided by 1.25 =	240
Title page/copyright page	2
Dedication page (blank on back)	2
Acknowledgments page (blank on back)	2
Blank pages to make chapters begin on recto (20 chapters, half needing a blank page)	10
Back matter - order form and sales hype for next upcoming title	2
Total number of pages	258

Most book printers work with *signatures* of 32 pages. A signature is the number of pages that are laid out together for printing, then folded as a group before being glued or sewn into place for binding into the book. A full signature is 32 pages, a half signature is 16 pages, and a quarter signature is 8 pages. As long as your page count is divisible by 8, it isn't a problem. If your page count is not divisible by 8, then you are faced with a decision. Either leave the extra pages blank at the end of the book, or ask the printer to make it come out even, without blanks.

The second option will get expensive, as it involves cutting and binding an odd number of pages. The first option is all right, you see it done all the time, but why waste those extra pages? Use them for something if you can.

If you've gotten ahead of us here, you may have done the math and figured out that our example of 258 pages is not divisible by 8. What to do?

Let's look at the options. You could drop the idea of having the chapters begin on recto pages. That cuts ten pages for a total of 248, a number that is divisible by 8. That might be the simplest answer.

If you divide 258 pages by 8, you'll find that it equals 32.25 signatures. That's only two pages over a number divisible by

8. See where you could eliminate two pages. Perhaps the dedication and acknowledgments could be combined on one page, thereby eliminating two pages easily.

Perhaps the order form at the back of the book is not really necessary. We put one in each of our books and find that we get very few orders directly from them. But if you do have a second book in the works, this is the best possible way to alert readers to it. If they liked your first book, they will want to know about any other titles by the same author or when the next book in the series is expected. If this particular novel is your one and only, you could probably eliminate that piece of back matter.

Keep in mind, too, that these numbers are approximate at this point. Until you have actually done the layout, printed it on your laser printer, and made all corrections, you won't know. Be prepared to make slight adjustments in the number of front and back matter pages once the typesetting is done. For now, anyway, use the page count you've come up with to get quotes from printers.

Another item you'll want the printing company to include in their bid is for extra dust jackets for a hardcover, or extra covers for a trade paperback. There are two reasons for having extra covers on hand.

It is inevitable that some books returned from stores will come back damaged. If your books are hardcover, usually the book is perfectly all right; the dust jacket will be the problem. It may have tiny tears or be slightly crushed on the edges, making it just a little too worn to be sold in a store. By having spare dust jackets on hand, you can simply replace the torn one with a fresh one and sell the book as new again, providing it doesn't have any other damage.

With softcovers, unfortunately you can't just replace the damaged cover. But those extra covers can be used in many ways for marketing, such as making up press kits, mailing direct as a large postcard, and making signs or posters for your book signings. Use your slightly damaged books for review copies or donate them to a library.

Extra jackets are extremely reasonable if you order them along with the book printing job. We pay about $75 for 500 extra full-color dust jackets. And the printer frequently has overruns, which they throw in at no charge. We've received as many as 1,000 extra jackets for the same price. Ask the printer to quote the cost for covers or jackets at the time they quote the book price.

Setting your cover price:

Pricing your book will be one of the most important decisions you make, and it must be done before the cover art goes to the printer because you need to have the price printed on the cover. So, how do you figure out what to charge?

Industry estimates have shown that a standard markup should be between five and eight times the production costs of your first print run. At the same time, you need to stay close to current pricing for books within your field. For instance, some how-to, textbooks, and educational books are priced much higher than eight times production costs because of the perceived value of the information contained within. Rarely does fiction fit this mold.

On the other hand, studies have shown that people usually don't pass up a book they really want to buy because it might be a dollar or two more than similar books. In fact, a book can be perceived to be of lesser quality or value if it carries a significantly lower price tag. At the time of this writing, hardcover fiction titles are ranging from around $18.95 on the low end to as much as $27.00 for bestseller "big" books. Check around. The review and bestseller list sections of *PW* show the cover price of each book listed. Look for books similar in content and length to yours to get some idea.

Keeping this in mind, there is a formula which you must

apply to pricing your own books to assure that you will make a profit. Choosing a price because another title in the same genre sells for that amount is not the way to do it.

First, you need to determine exactly what your production costs really are. You've received bids from printers by this time, and have probably decided which one you plan to work with. Here are some of the other things you need to take into consideration.

For this example, we'll say that you plan to print 3,000 books, hardcover, with four-color dust jackets.

Printer's bid (includes printing the dust jackets) $ 8,000
Typesetting (you did this yourself—if you paid for typesetting, you must include that figure here)   0
Cover art $ 1,000
Freight (this will vary depending upon the distance from the printing plant to you) $ 1,100
Total printing cost $10,100

Divide this cost by the 3,000 books and you come up with a cost per book of $3.37. Multiply this by the suggested factors above. Your book should be priced between $16.85 (5X cost) and $26.96 (8X cost). Look again at the books currently on the store shelves within your genre. What kind of average prices do you find? In the example above, these figures were taken from one of our own titles, and we ended up pricing the book at $21.95, which was fairly average for mystery hardcovers at that time. Going with the absolute low end price of $16.85 would have cost us $5.10 per book, or $15,300 on a sell-through of 3,000 books (assuming we sold them all at retail). Going to the high end price of $26.96 probably would have cost sales because at this time only the most well-known bestsellers were priced in that range.

When pricing, take a hint from established retailers. Studies have shown that consumers perceive $9.99 as significantly less than $10.00, $21.95 as less than $22.00. They are also more attracted to odd numbers than even: $21.95 rather than $21.96. Don't ask why.

What if your low end price (the 5X costs figure) comes out way too high? For instance, if your cost came out around $5.00 per book, so that when you multiplied it by five, you were looking at a cover price of $25.00. You've determined that all other hardcovers in your genre are selling at around $20. What should you do?

Your options are: 1) List yours at $25 anyway, in which case as an unknown author you probably won't sell many; 2) Look for ways to cut your production costs (by typesetting it yourself, getting bids from more printers, simplifying the cover art); or 3) Price it below 5 times markup, in which case it's unlikely you'll make a profit no matter how many books you sell.

Obviously, the smartest of these choices is to review your production costs. If you planned to have someone else typeset the book, reevaluate your decision about getting a laser printer and doing it yourself. Or get more bids from book printers. In our comparisons of a dozen or so companies, the prices varied quite a bit. Maybe you've just tried the more expensive ones. See if you can't get some more bids. Ask those printers you have contacted how they might suggest you cut costs. You might go with less expensive paper or binding. You could go with 2-color cover art, rather than 4-color process. The printing company can perhaps suggest some alternatives and can send you samples of what they plan to use so you can determine if it is acceptable.

TIP: If you plan to submit your camera-ready pages electronically, talk to your printer about his formatting requirements first.

Sending it to the printer

The pages are printed. The cover art is done. Your cover artist will have probably sent color proofs to you along the way, and will send the finished composite film directly to the book printer for you. You've ordered the Bookland EAN scanning symbol and have either sent it to the cover designer, or you have it in your possession and will need to send it to the book printer along with the typeset pages.

There are two ways to submit your book. Increasingly, printers are favoring the submission of books on disk. It's wise to check with the printer you've chosen to use as to format and requirements for doing it this way.

The old fashioned way, and one that still works fine, is to submit the typeset pages themselves. By this time, you have probably printed out the entire book at least two times. Make sure you have checked every page on the final copy with great care. The copy you send to the printer will be photographed, and the camera picks up everything. If you have a bit of blurry type, it will appear in every book. If there is a smudged fingerprint, that will be there too. Tiny flecks in the paper itself will show. Clean these up, either by reprinting the page or by using white correction fluid.

Look at every page. Check for tiny flaws and be sure that all page numbers, headers and footers are correctly placed. Once you are certain that the pages are in good shape, package them securely enough to mail. Placing stiff cardboard on both the front and back of the sheaf of paper and holding it all together with rubber bands works well. Be sure to include the EAN scanning symbol if you have not already sent it to the cover artist. And unless you have prior credit approval, this is the point at which you have to send the money for the job.

Be sure you've kept a printed copy for yourself, as well as your backup computer disks of the final version. We recommend sending the package via an overnight or two-day delivery service. Yes, it's more expensive, but after all the work you've put into this project, wouldn't it be heartbreaking to have the package get lost? The less time in transit the better chance of its arriving in good shape.

Plus, if you've been in contact with your print shop of choice since the bids all came in, they've probably put your job into the production schedule. A delay of a week will have far-reaching repercussions.

Once the printer has your job in hand, he may contact you with questions. Be available or risk delaying the job. One of the questions that will come up, if it hasn't already, is whether you want to review bluelines of your book. Bluelines are proofs that show exactly what your finished pages will look like. It is important that you review some, if not all, the blueline pages for your book. The purpose of bluelines is to catch errors in placement of text, pagination, location of any illustrations, etc. This is not the time to revise your writing or to spell-check. Those things should have been done long ago.

If your book has pictures, captions, illustrations, or characteristics other than plain text, you should review the entire book. Photos and their captions are easily misplaced or misnamed because the printer is not as familiar with the work as you are. In our case, with our books being straight text, we usually just review one signature. Look for headers, footers, page numbering, etc. In one instance, we found two pages out of sequence.

The printer will include an approval sheet with the bluelines. If everything is all right, a verbal okay is usually sufficient. But if there are any changes at all, make them in writing. On the approval sheet indicate any errors you found and ask them to either proceed with the job with the indicated changes, or if the changes are extensive, to resubmit new blues showing the changes. It is important that you review and return the bluelines as quickly as possible so you don't lose your place in the production schedule.

Well, your baby is out of your hands now. Can you just sit back for the next four to six weeks doing nothing?
Better read on.

Chapter 5

Getting Reviews

Now is a good time to catch your breath and double check that you've done all your preliminary work.

Did you send ABI forms to R.R. Bowker for *Books in Print*? Did you send new title information (on the forms they supplied) to Baker & Taylor, Ingram, Dustbooks, and any other distributors you plan to work with.

Remember, we suggested in chapter 3 that you set your pub date two to four months after the finished books are due from the printer. Here is one of the primary reasons why.

The major players in the book review business are *Publisher's Weekly, Library Journal, Booklist, Kirkus Reviews,* the *New York Times Book Review*, and the *Los Angeles Times*. (Their addresses are in the Appendix.) A review in one or more of these publications can go a long way toward giving your book a good sendoff. A rave review in one of these can send your sales soaring. Playing by their rules is the only way you can make it happen, and submitting your book the way they want it done will carry far more weight than having a certain ISBN number, an ample advertising budget, or any other advantage that the big publishers might have.

All the major industry review sources require review copies 3-5 months before the book's publication date. They want only "new" books, books that can be reviewed a month or more before the pub date. To get your book into the system, it must be there early. Barbara Hoffert, reviewer for *Library Journal* once told me, "It doesn't have to be pretty, it just has to be here early."

The big publishers send reviewers what are known as bound galleys. They are basically paperback versions of the finished book, with plain covers. Inside, there will be some sales information: Pub date, number of pages, ISBN, LCCN, cover price, publisher's name and address. There might also be some interesting information about the author, along with any advertising budget or tour information. Bound galleys are expensive, as much as $20 per copy.

Since you only need six copies to cover the major review sources, there are much less expensive ways to do this. Your other review sources can wait until you have finished books in hand.

Here's what we've done, and since every one of our published titles (so far) has been reviewed in at least one of the majors, we have to believe we're doing something right.

Make six complete copies of the typeset galleys you kept. We do this on our own copier at a cost of about 3¢ per page. Take the collated copies (it will be a sizeable stack of paper) to a good full-service copy shop.

Most shops offer several choices of binding. The plastic comb binding is the least expensive, but we prefer a channel bind or velo-bind. Most of these can be done for $3-$5 per book.

Have the copy shop make color copies of the front cover art and get one bound into the front of each set of galleys for a very effective presentation to your reviewers.

Find out which editor at each publication covers reviews in your genre. Send a bound copy to his or her attention along with a letter explaining the submission. Be sure to say that you are submitting these advance galleys for a book that is to be published in (whatever month). Mention if it is the author's first book, or give titles of books previously published by this author. You can also mention if you have an author tour planned or have an advertising budget for the book.

We've found that asking them to acknowledge the submission, even by sending back a postage paid card, gets little response. These people get hundreds of books each month, and they just won't take the time. All you can do is send off your galleys and hope for the best.

Oh, one final follow-up step you should follow. When you do have finished books from the printer, one of the first things you should do is to send one to each of these six main reviewers. Include a cover letter explaining that you had sent them bound galleys on (whatever date) and you wanted to follow-up with a finished book. This is proof to them that the book was actually published and does exist in finished form. Plus, it's a nice thank you gift for their taking the time to read your book in its unfinished form.

TIP: When submitting review copies, don't tell them that it's a self published book.

Using an editorial name

Another factor that may have contributed to our getting widely reviewed is that our books are not easily recognized as self-published. Reviewers are accustomed to receiving galleys and publicity packets from editors or publicists at larger publishing houses, not from authors.

You've already taken the first step by producing a first class book with great cover art and thorough proofreading. Sending your galleys and contact letters to the reviewers directly from the author, will alert them that you have published the book yourself.

If you are a one-man-show, it's good to have an alternate name for the person who will contact reviewers, write news releases, and contact bookstores. You can be that other person.

Many women simply use their maiden names, with perhaps their middle name or a female relative's name. Men can find some variation. You can sign a fictitious name statement with your bank so that you can sign checks with your editorial name, so that even those you have financial dealings with do not have to know that the company owner is you, the author.

Getting reviewed in other sources

Now you're going to call upon some of that research you did early on. If you have not already done so, you should enter the names and addresses of as many reviewers as you can come up with into a database. Many general reviewers can be found in *Literary Market Place*. Try to also locate as many names of reviewers as you can who specialize in your genre. Perhaps your writer's association has such lists, or you can find out who they are by reading reviews of other author's books in genre publications.

Write up a press release about your book. Use a journalistic style — you are the publicist touting the publishing company's newest title. If your book has any kind of news angle, now is the time to bring that out. Make the release catchy. This is the time to toot your own horn, making your book sound exciting. Mention any awards you might have won in the past or any other published works you have. Sell the sizzle and make readers eager to pick up your book.

At the bottom of the press release, offer a free review copy via a send-back form.

Also write a mock-up review of the book. This should also be written in journalistic format, like a reviewer would do after reading the book, although in this case it is more a telling of the story than an opinion piece. If the publication simply does not have the manpower to review every book itself, they may print your mock-up review.

Intrigue Press

Publishers of Mystery, Suspense, Adventure

Dear Reviewer,

It's every therapist's worst nightmare -- a client who commits suicide and blames incompetent therapy as the reason. In her debut novel *Secret's Shadow*, author Alex Matthews throws her protagonist, Cassidy McCabe, right into the middle of that exact situation.

Cassidy's life is already complicated enough: a cat with an attitude has adopted her as a housemate; the mob is demanding her ex-husband's whereabouts; she is struggling to pay her ex's back taxes; her charming fixer-upper house is deteriorating, and her malpractice insurance has lapsed. Even for an independent savvy woman of the 90s, finding the humor in her situation is sometimes a stretch.

When the dead client's black sheep brother approaches her to help prove that Ryan didn't kill himself, Cassidy knows she's asking for trouble. Ryan's brother, Zach, is trouble. Getting involved in the client's personal life is trouble. Trying to handle her legal problems without help from an attorney is trouble. But Cassidy persists, only to uncover a long buried secret whose shadow stretches across time -- and to find her own life in danger.

Now, if she can only resist her mother's pressure tactics, get her ex-husband out of her life, and get the mob to stop harassing her.

Author Alex Matthews is a therapist in private practice with her husband in Oak Park, Illinois. Matthews, who considers many female protagonists too masculine, set out to create an amateur sleuth possessing the strengths and insecurities of Everywoman. *Secret's Shadow* has already drawn high praise from well-known authors and will be our lead title for Spring.

To receive a copy of this exciting new mystery, simply call me or return the form below.

Sincerely,

Lee Ellison

YES, I'd like to read and share this intriguing new mystery. Please send a complimentary review copy of *Secret's Shadow*.

Name _____ Phone _____

Publication/Organization _____

Address _____

City/State/Zip _____

P.O. Box 456, Angel Fire, NM 87710   (505) 377-3474   fax (505) 377-3526

Sample Press Release

Terrorists Access America's Nuclear Weapons
in suspenseful new novel

Shiite Muslim terrorists with access to America's nuclear weapons? A master plan to destroy the eastern seaboard and cripple the U.S. Navy? -- Impossible?

* * *

The Gulf War has just ended. A British agent has fought his way through mine fields, exploding tanks and "friendly fire" from an American helicopter to deliver a terrifying message. A Shiite terrorist has been planted in deep cover aboard America's largest aircraft carrier, the nuclear-powered U.S.S. Venture. The plan -- to bring the world's greatest super-power to its knees while "the eyes of the world are watching."

Tom Barnes, one of the FBI's most successful black men, heads the National Security Council's Crisis Intervention Team. With his longtime partner, Frank Pierce, Tom's mission is to form a team to identify the terrorist and avert global disaster.

Tom recruits Navy Lieutenant Lee Curtis and operative Mike Young. Lee will maintain an apartment in Cannes, the Venture's Mediterranean port and the Crisis Intervention Team's base of operations. Mike Young will be stationed aboard the Venture in a high security position that allows him access to most of the ship's Secret and Top Secret areas.

Aboard the Venture, only

two men will know the true situation -- Captain James Halliday and First Class Petty Officer Matt Blackthorn, a third generation Navy man whose duties as a safe water inspector take him all over the massive ship.

When one of the team members dies under mysterious circumstances, the others know they must act quickly. But among a ship's crew of over five thousand men, how will they locate the terrorist? How will they unravel his plan before disaster strikes?

Tension builds among the team members as the Venture is assigned to circumnavigate the globe demonstrating its weapons capabilities in a Power for Peace gesture. The Crisis Intervention Team struggles to pinpoint the terrorist without arousing suspicions as the Venture changes location each day. Exotic ports come and go -- Sydney, Karachi, Rio de Janeiro -- while the Shiites set their plan in action.

New York harbor will be the Venture's last port -- its very last -- unless the team acts quickly. They know the terrorist is in place and they know he is capable of creating a nuclear incident.

Impossible?

Fans of Tom Clancy and Robert Ludlum will be drawn into this intricate plot of espionage and danger in Dan Shelton's debut novel.

* * *

Author Dan Shelton served as an Aviation Ordnanceman aboard the USS Enterprise during the Vietnam War, where assembling and arming weapons was his specialty.

Since leaving the military, he has had a 28 year career as a helicopter pilot. He has flown virtually every type of small helicopter in nearly every conceivable setting, from head-hunter territory in South America to the frozen tundra in Alaska.

During the 1980s he flew over 3,000 medical evacuation flights with the Flight For Life programs in both Denver and Las Vegas. The 1990s found him completing 10,000 helicopter tours on the island of Kauai, where he also did another stint for the US Navy as a member of the ordnance team at the Barking Sands Naval Facility.

He currently operates his own helicopter company and is working on his second novel.

* * *

Assault on the Venture
by Dan Shelton
ISBN 0-9643161-2-9
Hardcover, 256 pgs, $21.95

Contact:
Intrigue Press
P.O. Box 456
Angel Fire, NM 87710
505-377-3474

This review may be used in its entirety, or in an edited version, without further permission.

Sample Mock-up Review

Print the press releases on your company stationery, the mock-up review on plain paper, and mail these two items out to the reviewers on your list. Within a week or two, you should start receiving the requests for review copies. Save them in a folder until your books arrive. Any time you learn of more review sources in your genre, simply update these materials and send them to the new sources.

To Stamp or Not to Stamp:

When reading another well-known self publishing manual, we picked up a tip about marking review copies as such so they would not eventually find their way back into our stock as returns. It makes sense—you don't want to issue a credit memo for a book that you gave away in the first place, right? This was something we'd never considered with our first title, *Deadly Gamble*. So, when *Vacations Can Be Murder* came out, we had a rubber stamp made and diligently stamped the first half-dozen or so review copies with the wording "Review Copy, Not For Sale."

Within a few days, a reviewer from Albuquerque sent me a note. This man had given *Deadly Gamble* a wonderful review, one that had been reprinted in several publications. I had subsequently met him and found him to be a warm and friendly person with a genuine love of books and very supportive of small presses. He had been in the publishing business for over 30 years, retired from a major New York house, and had written reviews for many years. His note offered some advice from the reviewer's point of view. He suggested that I might not want to use the rubber stamp any more, and why. I pass his tips along so you can avoid the embarrassment I felt.

1. Only the smallest of kitchen table presses use this technique. Any reviewer in the know recognizes a stamped book as self-published.

2. Most reviewers work for no pay and the only reimbursement they get is to keep review copies for their collections.

3. Many reviewers will refuse to review a stamped book because they feel you have questioned their integrity by insinuating that they would try to sell the book. It may even go into the trash.

That was good enough for us. The rubber stamp went into the trash immediately.

Does this mean that you should meekly accept returns of books that may include advance copies you've sent to stores? No, that's a different matter. Here's what was suggested to me by a sales rep with a major publisher. The big publishers will usually have special books printed up for review by stores. They are usually a softcover version of a hardcover book; sometimes they are nothing more than bound galleys. In any case, they will have the words Advance Reading Copy printed on the cover.

Since we've already determined that bound galleys are much more expensive than finished books, you can accomplish the same thing quite easily. Make up a sticker—a computer label is fine— that says:

ADVANCE READING COPY
PLEASE PASS THIS BOOK AMONG YOUR STAFF

This does not offend by suggesting that they might try to get credit for the book later. You would easily recognize such a return, even if they attempted to remove the label. And it does make the effective suggestion that they read the book and have their employees do the same. Yes, they might sell the book to a customer. It's frequently done, especially by those dealers specializing in used books and collectibles. But, so what? Consider it additional promotion.

Reviews on the Net

The Internet and the various on-line services available today are burgeoning as places to talk about books. In addition to on-line bookstores, there are reader's groups, fan groups, and chat rooms where genre fans meet regularly to talk about what they read. Join in on the chat. Introduce yourself as a new author and tell a little about your book. Ask your friends to post favorable comments for you. While this is not exactly a review, it is a way to get your name and your book titles out to literally millions of people.

Of course, there are web sites that do run book reviews. Some are general and some genre specific. Browse them to learn about their format. You can usually post a message or e-mail the person in charge to find out how to go about sending copies of your book for review.

Can you expect sales over the Internet? It's hard to track exactly where some sales come from, particularly on the Internet unless you have a Web site with direct ordering capability. You can easily list your titles with any of the on-line bookstores. Although most of them do not stock every title they offer, they will order the books as their customers request them.

Any listing we print here will naturally be outdated before it is printed, but the Appendix lists some of the internet sites of which we are aware. Explore around, look for sites that focus on your genre. Chances are, your genre association newsletters will mention web sites that favor your titles. Be sure to check them out.

Some final thoughts on getting reviewed

Tens of thousands of new books are published every year. Reviewers are bombarded with so many choices that they cannot possibly cover them all. They, like booksellers and readers, must choose from an extremely vast field.

There are some things you can do to help yourself get into the competition. There are also some things that will keep you out of the competition. Don't be your own worst enemy.

1. Publish fiction in hardcover. Especially among the major review sources, the percentage of hardcovers that get reviewed is far greater than that of paperbacks. Trade paperbacks in fiction get almost no notice. For instance, an average issue of *Publisher's Weekly* reviews about 30-35 fiction titles. Of these, only three or four are trade paperbacks.

2. Send bound galleys early. Without enough time to get the book into their system, they won't even look at it. You are only shooting yourself in the foot if you send them a finished book after its publication date.

3. Follow up your bound galleys with a finished book as proof that it really exists.

4. Remember that critical first impression. Don't do your own cover art. Please leave this to the professionals. A good cover is well worth the tiny 30-50¢ per book added cost.

Chapter 6

Distribution

One of the least understood, at least by most authors, angles to the publishing business is the distribution system. That is, how the books get from the publisher to the stores. And most trade publishers give their authors very little idea how this works.

While some bookstores will order directly from the publisher, most of them, especially with titles from small presses, would rather order through a distributor or wholesaler.

Why?

Basically, because they don't know you. You are a small press with only one or two titles. Your author is an unknown. Most of the stores will want to start small, perhaps with only two or three copies of your book. If you set your terms and conditions according to our recommendation, that doesn't get them a very good discount. They like to be in the 40% range.

But they can order three copies of your title and three copies of someone else's title and a dozen of a best seller from their wholesaler, and be up there in the discount range where they want to be. Plus, they only have one invoice to pay, rather than one from each publisher, and they know the wholesaler will accept returns and make good on any damaged books.

What's the difference between a wholesaler and a distributor?

In the most basic terms, a wholesaler is an order taker.

They do not send sales reps into the stores; the stores have to know what titles they want and place orders for them. The two major wholesalers in this country are Baker & Taylor Books and Ingram Book Co.

Distributors

A distributor has commissioned sales reps who call on stores, present the available titles, and make a sales pitch to their customers, the stores. They then fill the orders they've received, either from stock they keep in their own warehouses, from the major wholesaler's stock, or from the publisher. There are dozens of distributors. Some of the larger ones are listed in the Appendix.

What does this mean to you, and which is better?

On the face of it, you would think working with a distributor is better. After all, they make the effort to go out and sell the books for you, right? Well, sometimes.

If you read the distributor's contract, here are some things to watch for.

Most of them will want an exclusive arrangement with you, the publisher. This means that you cannot accept orders directly from stores. All orders placed, even those that you generate yourself through your wholesalers, will go through the distributor and be commissionable to them.

You can find yourself giving away as much as 65-70% of the cover price of your book. After all, the bookstore gets their discount, the wholesaler will get a percentage, and the distributor will get a percentage on top of that. Now you know why we suggested a 5-8 times cost markup when pricing your books.

Under most distributor agreements, you the publisher will be responsible for all advertising and promotion of your titles. Yes, your distributor will list your titles in their catalog and will make sales calls to the stores. Don't count on this to make many sales for you, though. Request a copy of a distributor's catalog sometime. Most of the titles listed get anywhere from a few lines to (maybe) a quarter page. The catalog will list hundreds of titles from dozens of publishers. Unless you've done something to draw attention to your books, both with the distributor and with the bookstore, it will not get much representation.

You will also be responsible for shipping a supply of your books to the distributor's warehouse and insuring the stock while on their premises. You can be more assured of getting your money from a distributor than from a store, since distributors go out of business far less often than bookstores, and they are responsible for collecting from the stores. However, you can plan on an extra 60-120 days to collect your money.

So much for the pluses and minuses. The big question will be whether you can even get a distributor. With the increasing number of small presses out there, distributors can afford to be more choosey about whom they will represent. It is especially difficult for one-book publishers to find representation. Still, it doesn't hurt to contact some distributors and talk to them. Send them copies of your books. See what they have to offer.

We found that after publishing our fourth title, the distributors started approaching us. Be careful, though. One distributor wrote to us, enclosing a contract that was very simple. They wanted to begin representing us immediately. All we had to do was sign the contract and send them ten complimentary copies of each title for their sales reps. The contract called for exclusive representation and we'd never heard of this distributor, so I looked them up in *Literary Market Place*. There was no listing, so I wanted to know a bit more before sending them 40 books, over $800 retail value. I wrote them back, thanking them for considering us, and asking how they found out about us and a few questions about their company, such as: How long had they been in business?

What territory did they cover? Would they represent us to the chain stores as well as the independents? All very natural questions, I thought. We never received a reply or heard another word from them. Maybe they decided we were too small potatoes for them. Or maybe they simply wanted 40 free books?

Wholesalers

As we mentioned, the two major wholesalers in the country are Baker & Taylor and Ingram. They each have some different rules to play by, but it is not that difficult to work with them.

Baker & Taylor's system is easy to get into. We recommend that you do this early on, preferably while your first book is at the printer. Call 908-218-3803 and ask for the new publisher packet. This information will explain their billing and shipping procedures. Two crucial items that must be on your book to be included in Baker & Taylor's system are the ISBN and EAN Bar Code. They will not handle titles without these.

There is a $100 one-time fee for being added to their database. You fill out a vendor questionnaire and a new title information form for each book. B & T requests a 55% discount, payment due in 90 days, freight paid by publisher. You can set your own terms, but these are the guidelines they suggest. We went along with the 55% discount and 90 day payment terms, but worked it out so they pay freight on orders of fewer than 10 books. Since Baker & Taylor services both bookstore and library accounts, it is well worth the small fee and the time to get established with them.

Ingram is the largest wholesaler in the country and usually the source of choice for bookstores. They have two programs for publishers, the regular program whereby they keep an inventory of your books in stock, and the Greenlight program in which Ingram places orders from publishers as they receive orders from customers. Their selections committee reviews all new titles and decides which program they will put you into. A small publisher can usually only get into the Greenlight program. Still, it's worth doing in light of the fact that most bookstores will call Ingram first. Once you have some impressive sales data to show, you can be upgraded to the regular program.

To get into their system, write Wanda Smith, Publisher Relations Manager, Ingram Book Company, PO Box 3006, La Vergne, TN 37086-1986 or call 615-793-5000 for their new publisher information. They will send a vendor questionnaire and new title forms. Their requested terms are the same as those of Baker & Taylor. Ingram will not pay freight on any quantity of books, and in fact will penalize you if you add freight to an invoice. We learned this the hard way.

With either of these major wholesalers, it is very important that you follow their billing instructions to the letter, if you plan to get paid. They are both good at paying on time, provided you follow instructions.

Both major wholesalers offer additional publisher promotion opportunities, including flyers that go out with all orders to bookstores, telemarketing of your titles to stores who call to order, and more. Check with your account rep to find out more.

TIP: When working with wholesalers, it is imperative that you follow their billing and shipping instructions. Failure to do so will cost you money and time.

Selling directly to stores

We mentioned reasons that stores might not want to order directly from a small publisher but some will, and there are a few things you will need to know.

Stores will typically order from you in one of three ways. Many will place an order using their store Mastercard or Visa and if you have merchant status to accept those cards, this makes it easy. You get your money immediately and can ship the books with confidence that you have been paid.

In the book trade, there is another commonly used form of prepayment called the STOP order. This stands for Single Title Order Plan. The store will send you an order, often for only one or two books, along with a check. Most publishers will allow the store a discount, even on a single book order done this way, because of the fact that they are being paid immediately. (See our Terms & Conditions form) The enclosed check is made out to you and the amount is left blank. You bill the order with the appropriate discount, add shipping charges, and fill in the amount on the check. Again, you have payment in advance and can ship the books immediately.

If you are going to extend open credit to an account, it only makes good business sense to run a credit check. Every publishing company has to decide for themselves how to handle this. We allow an open account to virtually any store in an amount of $100 or less. This allows them to buy five books, which is the typical order, get their 40% discount, and take 30 days to pay. So far, we've not been burned.

If a store wants to place an order larger than $100, we insist upon a credit check. We designed this basic credit information form, which they fill out and return to us. We follow up on the credit references they give, either by phone or mail, before extending credit.

While wholesalers insist upon 90 day terms, we extend only 30 day terms to stores. Our computer software will print out statements at the end of each month and we send them to all accounts with open invoices as they become due. For instance, if the purchase was made on January 5, the invoice becomes due on February 5. We would not normally send a statement on February 1st to this account because the invoice

Bookstore Account Application

FIRM NAME _____ D&B # _____

MAILING ADDRESS _____ PHONE _____

CITY, ST, ZIP _____ COUNTY _____

SHIPPING ADDRESS (IF DIFFERENT) _____

PRINCIPAL(S) _____ BUYER _____

REFER ALL FINANCIAL MATTERS TO: _____ YEARS IN OPERATION _____

NUMBER OF FULL-TIME SALES PEOPLE _____ ANNUAL SALES $ _____

IS BUSINESS A CORPORATION, PARTNERSHIP OR PROPRIETORSHIP? _____

IS BUSINESS A DIVISION OR SUBSIDIARY OF ANOTHER CORPORATION? _____

IF YES, CORPORATION NAME _____ CITY, ST _____

BANK NAME _____ CONTACT _____

ADDRESS _____ PHONE _____

ACCT # _____ LOAN # _____

LINE OF CREDIT $ _____ SECURED _____ UNSECURED _____

CERTIFICATE OF RESALE # _____

TRADE REFERENCES (PUBLISHERS OR WHOLESALERS PREFERRED)

NAME _____ PHONE _____

ADDRESS, CITY ST, ZIP _____

NAME _____ PHONE _____

ADDRESS, CITY, ST, ZIP _____

NAME _____ PHONE _____

ADDRESS, CITY, ST. ZIP _____

We the undersigned understand and agree to the Terms and Conditions set forth on the attached sheet. In case of default, the undersigned will be responsible for reasonable attorney fees incurred by Intrigue Press. Legal action, if required, will be pursuant to and conducted in the courts of New Mexico.

Signed _____

(Principal only)

Date _____

Office Use Only:
Date approved _____
By _____
Acct # _____

Complete and return to : Intrigue Press, P.O. Box 456, Angel Fire., NM 87710

Credit Application for Bookstores

is not actually due yet. But, come March 1st, if it is still unpaid, they will definitely get a statement of account. The program will automatically print increasingly urgent messages at the bottom of each statement as the invoices get older. By 90 days, if the invoice was due in 30, we get on the phone.

As we mentioned earlier, many businesses have gone broke because of accounts receivable that have gotten out of control. Don't let this happen to you. Watch your accounts carefully, send invoices and statements according to established business practices, and make collection calls as necessary to be sure you are paid on time. Watch the bookseller news items in *PW*. They frequently list the names of stores that are having financial problems or going out of business.

Seller beware!

Chapter 7

Advertising, Publicity, and Promotion

By this time, if you've talked to any other published authors, you've figured out that publicity and promotion are a necessary part of every successful author's life. Even those writers published by the big guys are usually surprised to find that their publishers do very little to promote most of their authors. The author himself must take the responsibility for getting his name out there.

As your own publisher, your company can make a bigger push for each book than you could ever expect to get if you were just a tiny fish in the big pond at a trade publisher.

The basic marketing strategy

One fundamental that a fiction publisher needs to understand is the concept of three-level marketing.

What do we mean?

Simply this: you need to market on three levels, to readers, to bookstores, and to your wholesaler/distributor network. Fiction buyers, unlike those looking for how-to's or self improvement, order very few books directly from the publisher. You need the wholesalers, distributors and bookstores to get your books into your reader's hands. Always keep this in mind.

If you market directly to readers, that's fine. But if they

can't get your book in their local store, through a book club or established mail order catalog, you've lost them. They'll buy another author's book because it's convenient.

If you market to bookstores, unless you can generate loads of *handselling* enthusiasm, where store personnel recommend your book to their customers, the book will simply sit on the shelf if readers don't know about it.

And if the bookstore can't get your book from its favorite wholesaler, the book won't be on the shelf when the reader comes in and requests it.

We'll talk more about these strategies in the chapter on Making a Name for Yourself as an Author. For now, just keep in mind that your marketing must include all three levels.

TIP: **Introduce yourself to bookstore personnel wherever you go. Leave postcards or pens and a business card.**

What works and what doesn't

Having polled several dozen fiction self-publishers, we came up with some interesting answers about what works and what doesn't work when it comes to advertising, publicity, and promotion.

The *most* effective strategies cited by the publishers we polled were (in no particular order):

Direct mail to libraries and bookstores
Ads in genre magazines
Radio interviews (when the topic is a timely one)
Speaking to schools and clubs on topics relating to the book
Attending conferences, networking
Targeting an audience (i.e. therapists, when the main character is a therapist)
Putting out GREAT books!

Let's take a closer look at each of these ideas and how you can implement them yourself.

Direct mail to libraries and bookstores

In Chapter 5, we mentioned the importance of developing your mailing lists. By this time, you should have done your research and located plenty of bookstores and libraries, which you've entered into your database. Or you've rented mailing lists in these market segments.

Design a flyer to hype your book.

1. Start with a catchy heading, something that poses a question or ties your book into a current news item or makes your plot or characters sound irresistible.

2. Include a copy of the cover art.

3. Sell the benefit—this is paramount in any type of sales. You must tell the customer what you can do *for them*. With bookstores and libraries, they want to know why people will buy or check out this book. If one of your reviews mentions the book's great cover, quote that. It tells the bookseller that their customers will pick it up. Libraries base their purchasing decisions almost completely on reviews, so quote them liberally. With readers of fiction, the benefit is entertainment value. Capsulize your plot in a couple of very tight, catchy sentences. Make every word count.

4. Give ordering information. If your titles are available through major wholesalers or distributors, be sure to mention this (review Chapter 6 on how to get your books into the distribution system). If you don't have a distributor, at least tell the recipients how to order directly from you and include an order form.

Work on your flyer design and print out a camera-ready original on your laser printer. There are some wonderful books available on writing advertising copy that sells product. Some

Vacations Can Be Murder!

"Vacations mean different things to different people. There's the planning, the packing, the anticipation. Then there's the late arrival, the sunburn, the fuzzy pictures. In my case, add a romance with a good-looking pilot and fourteen stitches in the back of my skull."
— Charlie Parker

Charlie's last case left her tired and emotionally drained, so her office staff convinces her to schedule a vacation to Kauai. Her first day on the island, Charlie takes a helicopter tour. When she and the pilot spot a dead body lying on the rocks of the rugged Na Pali coast, Charlie's vacation takes a turn for the *deadly*.

The second Charlie Parker mystery, October, 1995

- ➪ Author Tour
- ➪ Author appearances at selected mystery conferences
- ➪ Media Campaign
- ➪ National Ad Campaign in *Mystery Scene, Mystery Week* and others
- ➪ Direct mailing to Sisters in Crime membership
- ➪ Same day shipping on orders direct from publisher
- ➪ FREE sales aids— Bookmarks, Pens, Display Covers
- ➪ FREE article clips and reviews for your newsletter
- ➪ Signed copies on request

Don't forget backlist! Stock up now on Deadly Gamble, *the first Charlie Parker mystery*

Available through Baker & Taylor, Ingram, Brodart, Gannon, and other wholesalers, or directly from Intrigue Press. STOP purchasing available.

Vacations Can Be Murder
by Connie Shelton
ISBN 0-9643161-1-0
LCCN 95-77210
Hardcover, 216 pages, $21.95

Deadly Gamble
by Connie Shelton
ISBN 0-9643161-0-2
LCCN 94-79216
Hardcover, 216 pages, $21.95

Intrigue Press
P.O. Box 456
Angel Fire, NM 87710
505-377-3474   fax 505-377-3526
Orders call 1-800-99-MYSTERY

Advertising flyer for bookstores or libraries

of these are listed in the Appendix. If you have a scanner, you can make excellent printable halftones of your book cover to insert in the appropriate spot on the flyer. If you don't have a scanner, a photocopy will work, provided you do not reduce it so many times that you lose quality. Simply cut out the copy and paste it onto your flyer original.

You can take the camera-ready copy for your flyer to a copy shop if you can find a good rate. Or you can run them off on your own home-office copier. We've done this with literally thousands of flyers with good success. Compare your copy costs (price of paper and toner per copy) with the rate you can get at the copy shop. If their price is the same or less, you might as well put the wear and tear on their machine rather than yours.

Now, what else can you include in your mailing piece that will make it stand out from the rest?

Color postcards of your book cover are an excellent means of contact. You can send one of those extra dust jackets to a printer who specializes in postcards and get beautiful full-color cards of your cover. Have them print an excerpt from your cover copy or some favorable blurbs or reviews on the back, and you have a wonderful mailing tool. We pay about $500 for 5,000 full color cards. It's a small amount for the many ways they can be used to promote your book. Tuck one into each bookstore and library mailing along with the flyer.

We've also used various advertising specialty products to make our mailing stand out from the crowd. Ballpoint pens imprinted with the book title, author's name, ISBN, and our toll-free ordering number have worked great for us. Other inexpensive products that can be imprinted with any information you want and are flat enough to mail in a regular envelope include: buttons showing your book cover, letter openers, magnets, 6-inch rulers, and stickers. If you can afford to spend a little more, you can get personalized calculators (for a book with a financial angle), sunglasses (for a beach novel or one set in a tropical locale), mini tape measures ("measure" the success of this book!) and dozens of others. You can bet that an item like this, mailed in a padded bag with your flyer, will get opened and looked at. It's easy for people to throw away envelopes of paper, but a usable item will keep your message in front of them for a long time. Some sources of ad specialty products are listed in the Appendix.

About Bulk Mailing

There are different schools of thought on using bulk mail to contact potential customers. Some contend that today's busy business owner is so bombarded with junk mail that most of it ends up in the trash without a glance. On the other hand, if you can make your mailing piece stand out, it will get opened and bulk mail is the least expensive way to reach your targeted audience with something that they will keep.

Contact your post office to learn more about using bulk mail. They will provide you with their guide, called Third Class Mail Preparation, and the necessary applications.

In a nutshell it works like this. You get a bulk mail permit (renewable yearly) from the post office and they assign you a bulk mail permit number. This must appear on all your mailing pieces in a specified format. You must mail at least 200 identical pieces at a time. You can mail up to 2 ounces for the minimum rate (a great way to include those little giveaway items). Rates vary depending on the amount of sorting and barcoding you can do yourself, but even the highest bulk rate is about 30% less than First Class.

Downside: bulk mail takes 2-3 weeks to arrive at all destinations nationwide versus the 4-5 days for first class. But unless your book will be outdated in those two extra weeks, why not?

Time the mailing of your packet to bookstores to arrive during your publication month if possible. With libraries, timing isn't so critical. They make their buying decisions based largely on favorable reviews in trade publications such as *Publishers Weekly, Library Journal*, and *Booklist*, with reviews in smaller publications and newspapers carrying secondary weight. They are not easily swayed by publisher hype, so you would be better off waiting until you have some good reviews from outside sources to quote before approaching this market. This might be two or three months after publication, but that's okay.

Co-op mailings

Several publisher organizations offer co-op mailings to bookstores and libraries. They will always tell you how many pieces they plan to mail and the cost for including your piece in the mailing. The price may look attractive, but there are some other questions you should ask. For example:

- How many other flyers will be in the same envelope with ours?
- What genre will the other pieces cover?
- Will the mailing be targeted to fiction buyers? Non-fiction buyers? Not targeted at all?

If possible, get them to send you a piece from a previous mailing they sent to the same list you intend to mail to. What does the envelope look like? Is it appealing? Does it include wording on the outside that will make the receiver want to open it? Or is it generic white?

Look inside. Are all the flyers similar in quality? Are they similar to what you intended to supply? If your piece will be black print on a colored paper while everyone else's is full-color glossy, yours will seem inferior before it's even read.

Are all the pieces appropriate to the same buyer at the store or library? If yours is the only fiction flyer and the packet gets directed to the non-fiction buyer, chances are good that your piece will not make its way to the person who really needs to see it.

While co-op mailings can be a less expensive way to get your message out to a great number of names, just be sure it's really getting there. Our two experiences with co-op mailings were that they did pull some orders, but not nearly as many as our own mailings which were directed to the correct genre buyer and enclosed in our own distinctive envelope with the mystery logo in the corner.

TIP: Handselling by bookstores is probably the fiction writer's greatest ally.

Advance Reading Copies

In Chapter 5, we touched briefly on the subject of Advance Reading Copies or ARCs. These are complimentary books sent to bookstores before the publication date. The idea is to get store personnel to read the book, order it, and recommend it to their customers. Naturally, this will work best if you do some homework first and target those booksellers who are partial to your type of book. It won't do much good to send your romance novel to a mystery bookstore, or your western to one whose specialty is sci-fi and fantasy.

You will find the booksellers most interested in your genre through your writer's organizations. Read your newsletters carefully. Pay attention to the special genre issues of *Publisher's Weekly*. In researching their articles on certain genre trends, *PW* frequently interviews bookstore owners to get their opinions. Track down addresses for these stores and add them to your mailing list.

Obviously, you can't afford to send a free book to every bookstore in the country. So, how do you decide who gets a book and who merely gets flyers and catalogs? The simplest first step you can take is to target your mailing list. In our database, we have names and addresses of several thousand bookstores. Of these, we have researched and found that approximately 100 or so specialize in mysteries or have large mystery collections.

We created a field in the database called "genre specialist" and we tag each mystery store with a YES in this field. We can easily sort on this field to find just those stores that are likely to show more interest in our titles. These will be the stores to get ARCs.

Another way to determine which stores might get ARCs is to look for the special interest angle. How about targeting stores in the author's hometown? Or the town where the story takes place? Many stores, including the large chains like Borders, Barnes & Noble, Bookstar, Books-a-Million, etc., will have a prominent section featuring books by local authors. They may also have a section called "Recommended Books" or "Our Favorite Picks" or something similar. If you can get someone in the store to read and recommend your book, it can draw many more sales by being in this section.

Use your database's sort feature to get the addresses of stores by geographical area.

If you end up with lots of stores specializing in your type of books, and you simply can't afford to send free books to all of them, consider splitting up the list. Mail copies to half the list now and the rest of them in a couple of months, after you've generated some money to pay for the mailings. Mail copies of your first title to part of the list and wait until your second title comes out to reach the rest of the list.

Look for ways to keep your cost down in mailing review copies. We ship all orders by UPS because it is faster than the Postal Service's book rate, and the packages can be traced. But with review copies, you can't charge the postage to the receiver, so it might make sense to save some money by using the Special Fourth Class or "Book Rate" offered by the Post Office. Our average cost for one book is $3.00 by UPS, $1.74 by book rate. When sending out 50 to 100 review copies, this difference is sizeable.

After sending your ARCs to stores, it's a good idea to follow up. If you have the time, phone calls to selected stores can pay off. Develop your approach, as any good telemarketer would. Inquire about whether they received the complimentary book. Mention some of the marketing you are doing on behalf of the book, such as author appearances, advertising in genre publications, direct mailings to genre fans. (Tell them what *you* are doing to promote sales in *their* store.) Then don't forget to ask for an order. There's no sense in placing a nice, chatty phone call if you don't make it result in orders.

You can also follow up with stores by mail. Personalize each letter. Mention the free copy you sent, list the benefits to them of carrying the title in their store, and again, ask for the order. List your wholesalers and/or distributors, along with your phone number so they can order direct.

TIP: Don't run paid advertising unless you know it reaches your genre fans.

Ads in genre magazines

Paid advertising can be very expensive so you would do well to do your homework carefully and target only those publications which will directly reach your readers.

Once your publishing company is established in databanks nationwide, you will receive all sorts of solicitations for your advertising dollar. Whatever you decide to do, start small and target, target, target.

If your readers are sci-fi fans, we'd bet that few of them read *Publisher's Weekly*. Look instead for the magazines your readers read. In our field, mystery and suspense, there are literally dozens of fanzines and newsletters. Through your genre writers organizations, you'll start to hear about the ones that pertain to you. Add the names of these publications to your database.

How do you know if a particular publication is for you?

Under your publisher name, request a sample copy and their advertising rates. Browse the magazine carefully. Look for ways to get free publicity first.

Do they run book reviews? It's much easier to get reviewed within your genre than in the national trade publications, and many of them run reviews as much as a year after the book is published. If you missed the mark with *Publisher's Weekly* or *Library Journal* or the *New York Times*, there's still hope. Send the genre magazine a review copy of your book. A review is free advertising.

Do they run feature stories about authors? Many of these small mags don't have many staff writers and will actually welcome an interview that you've written yourself. You can do a simple Q & A format, asking yourself questions and providing the answers. Or a narrative style interview is equally easy to do. Check to see what they've already published, and follow that format. Don't expect pay, just free exposure.

Check out the advertising. Do they have display ads? What are the rates? We run a half-page ad in every issue of *Mystery Scene* magazine for less than $200 per issue. A third- or quarter-page is even more reasonable. The circulation of these genre magazines may be small (compared to *PW* or the *NY Times*) but so are the rates, and you are reaching *your* readers. It makes more sense to reach 8,000 people dedicated to your genre than a million general readers, only a few thousand of whom might be interested in your genre (at ten times the price, or more).

If you do opt for paid advertising, prepare the camera-ready artwork yourself on your laser printer. From your ideas file, pull out some ads you found particularly effective. Borrow ideas about layout and typestyle. By sending your own camera ready copy, you know what you'll get. If you merely provide information and trust the magazine to do the layout, insist upon seeing a proof before it goes to press. Check the proof carefully, especially the numbers like ISBN and price. Mark any errors and mail or fax it back to them. Don't give changes verbally.

Never send money and ad copy to a magazine you've never seen. We got the name of one that purported to be a mystery magazine, but when the sample magazine arrived it turned out that they were much more geared toward blood-and-guts horror than anything we publish. Not an image we wanted for ourselves.

There are a few ways you can get mentioned in the major trade magazines at reasonable cost. Again, target your audience. We mentioned that *PW* regularly runs features on various genre. The mystery writers group, Sisters in Crime, takes out a multi-page ad in the mystery issue. Individual members with published books can pay for listing their titles, effectively sharing the cost of a much larger ad than any of us could do on our own. The cost per title listing is only around $40.

Some of the publisher organizations also contract for shared space in *PW* and *Library Journal* at reduced rates to members. Weigh the cost vs. whether or not these ads will reach your targeted audience. Use paid advertising only when you feel you'll reach *your* buyers.

Don't overlook the chance for some free publicity in these big publications. As we mentioned earlier, watch the Call for Information section in *PW* and send your latest news. A columnist will probably call you if the magazine plans to use your information. Be ready with some insightful comments.

Radio Interviews

An author interview on the radio or TV can be one of the best free publicity opportunities you can get. Unfortunately, you'll find that most of these programs are not interested in fiction writers.

How can you get them interested?

Creating a news angle for your story is a must. You can't possibly write a book geared toward a news story, because by the time you finish the book, get it published, and out into the stores, it will be yesterday's news. So, you have to look at what you've already written and try to figure out what kind of timely connection you can make.

We mentioned a small press in Colorado who had a title that dealt with spouse abuse. Written as a historical novel, the story was about the protagonist's ways of dealing with her problem during a time in history when this topic was not talked about. The book was actually published nearly a year before the O.J. Simpson case, but the author was able to get quite a few radio interviews because the topic suddenly became timely. She sold out her first print run and went into a second printing.

Look for a news angle. Has your character dealt with a problem that's being talked about? Does the location fit into the news somehow? Does the plot parallel a recent news story? Do you deal with a current social issue such as environmentalism, feminism, pollution?

Once you find that angle, develop a press release that presents it in a fresh way. Talk shows, especially the major ones, are bombarded with press releases from potential guests. Think of a way to make yours different. Include quotes from an expert in the field if you can get them. Mail or fax the press release out as soon as the news angle breaks — they all want to be first with the story.

Be persistent. Follow up with them and don't stop following up until you have a firm no.

Sometimes your local TV and radio stations are willing to do interviews, particularly if you have an upcoming booksigning to tie in to, even if there is no particular news angle other than "local author makes good." These are often just 3-5 minute spots, but anything helps. The first time I appeared on television to promote a signing, it happened that two friends from the distant past happened to catch the broadcast and came by the signing. They hadn't even been aware that I had a book published. It was good to meet with them again, and the visit resulted in the sale of more books.

Speaking engagements

Once you've written a book, you become an expert in the minds of many people. Speaking engagements become relatively easy to get. Check with the Chamber of Commerce in your town. Many have speaker's bureaus, where organizations go to find speakers for luncheons, dinners, meetings, and conventions.

Or you can contact different organizations directly, via personal contacts you may have in the business world or through a mailing. Some of them will offer a small honorarium, but even those who don't will often let you sell books at the back of the room.

Another great speaking opportunity for fiction writers is in libraries. Many have regular times when they feature certain genre authors. Plan a short talk on writing or a reading from your book, then take questions from the audience. For many readers, it will be the first time they've ever talked to an author. Many libraries will allow you to sell books at the back of the room, or will offer to sell your book through their Friends of the Library organization.

Baker & Taylor offers a free publication called *Authors in Libraries*, which lists libraries nationwide that are particularly geared toward sponsoring author appearances. Write to Baker & Taylor, P.O. Box 6920, Bridgewater, NJ 08807-0920 or call 908-218-3893 to get a copy.

Establishing a Keylist

One of the most important ways in which you can establish a name for yourself as an author within your genre is by making and sending regular notices of your activities to a Keylist. What do we mean by Keylist?

This is a list of those organizations or people who can aid in getting the word out to many others. Make a list of all the writing organizations you belong to, along with the name and address of their newsletter editor. Most organizations have a newsletter column featuring its member's newsworthy activities. You might include on your Keylist the newsletters of any professional, fraternal, or social organizations to which you belong. Include your contact people at the book wholesalers or distributors you plan to work with.

Now, the key to making this list work for you is by staying in regular contact with them. Try to come up with something to tell them every month or two. Your first notice can be the exciting news of the publication of your first novel by XYZ Publishing (or whatever your publishing company's name is). Make it sound like this company has bought your book. This is probably not the time to tell them that you are self-publishing.

In another month or two, send notice of your gala pre-publication party. After that, keep them apprised of your book-signings, readings, or other speaking engagements. You can notify them before the event and then again after it is over.

Some publications are so eager to fill space that they will use everything you send. Others will fit in what they can. At any rate, the point is to get your name out in front of your intended audience and your fellow writers as often as possible.

Networking at conferences

After joining writers organizations pertinent to your genre, you should start to hear about genre conferences. These events are a wonderful opportunity to sell books and, even better, to help establish your name as an author.

Offer to be a speaker or appear on a panel. This is one of the best ways to promote your book (subtly). There is something about meeting an author, hearing her talk about her book, and having the chance to get the book signed, that appeals greatly to genre fans.

You'll also get a chance to meet booksellers who specialize in your genre. Take advantage of this. Introduce yourself and offer to sign any stock copies of your book. If they don't happen to have your book in stock, offer to sell them some from the supply you brought with you. Tell them a little about the book and give them a postcard or pen with ordering information. Be sure to mention if it's your first novel — many of them are looking for new authors.

If they decline, be gracious about it. It could be that they feel they are overstocked right now. If you are polite and gracious, they will remember that. If you act obnoxious and rude, they will remember that, too. Offer to leave them some extra postcards or pens that they can hand out to their customers. Tell them they can order after the show and offer them the same discount terms your regular bookstores get. Chances are, before the end of the conference, you'll have made new friends, and they will try some of your books.

The formats of conferences vary. Some will have multiple booksellers on the premises, so attendees can visit the book room, get your book, and have it signed immediately. Others will have one bookstore who hosts the conference and invites authors to their store, away from the conference, for a signing that they have advertised to the public. You'll soon get the hang of it after you've done a couple of events.

Networking with other authors is another great benefit to attending conferences. If you've done your pre-publication homework, sending regular notices to your Keylist, the people in the genre should have already heard of you before your first conference.

I started my Keylist contacts about three months before my first book came out. When I attended my first conference during my publication month, I was amazed at how many times, when introducing myself to fans, booksellers, and other authors, I met with the reaction, "Oh, yes, I've heard of your book." By the second year, attending the same conference, I was greeted by some of the big name authors in the genre like an old friend. In addition to being a heady feeling, I began to get included in dinners and social gatherings and to get invited as a speaker to other events.

In the book business, as in others, contacts are everything.

Should you tell them you are self-published? That's your call. For some reason, when you tell someone you have a book coming out, the first question seems to be, "Who's your publisher?" I never figured out why it matters, but I would answer by giving the name of my publishing company. Naturally, they'd never heard of it and then the questions would begin. Where are they located? Who are they? Who is your editor?

Personally, I'm not comfortable dodging that many questions, so I started admitting right out that I'm my own publisher. Usually, this brings on another rash of questions (at least they are questions I can answer honestly) and lots of curiosity. I've found that most writers are intrigued with the idea of maintaining complete control by doing your own publishing (especially those that have been burned by a larger publisher), and they are very friendly about the whole thing. Many of them will be interested in the process of publishing and you can steer them to this book as a guide to finding the answers.

Targeting a non-traditional audience

How about looking for other audiences? You certainly don't have to be limited to selling your books to genre fans. You just need to find a way to get those other people interested in your book.

Again, you need to look for an angle. Does your lead character have a profession shared by lots of people? Doctor, lawyer, baker, chief? Our Cassidy McCabe mystery series by Alex Matthews features a protagonist who is a psychotherapist. Because this therapist's clients figure prominently in the plots of the stories, and the therapist's own decision-making and lifestyle are all part of the stories, we felt these books might be of interest to therapists nationwide. Although these might not be people who would naturally walk into a bookstore looking for a novel whose main character is a therapist, they would surely be intrigued when they read our ad copy which begins, "It's every therapist's worst nightmare," and proceeds to give a brief synopsis of the story.

So, how do we reach them? We target them by profession. Whenever the author, herself a therapist, is planning a speaking engagement or booksigning, we get names of private practice therapists and clinics in the area. Postcards of the book cover go out to them, announcing the time and place of the author appearance. We send notices to therapist professional groups for their newsletters and to post on the bulletin boards in clinics. Think creatively—you can come up with some ideas, too.

Does your plot put your characters into a new milieu? Any setting that delves deeply into another world can work. Arthur Hailey's novels are an excellent example. He looked closely at such industries as automobile production, hotel management, and hospitals. Eileen Dreyer, a suspense author who also wrote romances under the name Kathleen Korbel, was formerly a trauma room nurse. Many of her books are set in hospitals, and her own years of experience lend chilling authenticity to her tales of suspense. Look to nurses and hospital workers, as well as others interested in the subject, to be readers of those types of books.

Locale can be another drawing card. If your story takes place in a real location (my mysteries are set in Albuquerque, New Mexico), you have an immediate interest from people who like to see their town in print. The local newspapers are very likely to review the book.

Many times they will use the local setting angle in a feature story. My husband and I got a full page feature story in a regional newspaper because the reporter was intrigued that we are both authors and we met in a romantic setting (I used this setting in my second novel, *Vacations Can Be Murder*). We were depicted as the sweetheart couple for the Valentine issue. You cannot buy that kind of advertising.

Starting an author newsletter

If you have written several books, starting an author newsletter is an excellent way to keep your name visible to your readers.

Several well-known mystery authors, such as Carolyn Hart, Jean Hager, and Carole Nelson Douglas have created beautiful newsletters. Check within your genre and you'll probably find others who've done the same.

To be effective, a newsletter needs to follow some guidelines:

Publish at least three times a year. Any less often than that, and your newsletter will be forgotten between issues. Quarterly is better, every two months if you have enough "news" to report and enough money.

It should contain something that is "news." This can be news of your newest book, a listing of your signing schedule, or something newsworthy that has happened to you.

Establish a format, or a "look" that remains constant in every issue. This is important in making your newsletter identifiable to your readers. When it arrives in the mail, they should know right away who it is from.

Another good reason for establishing a format is for the ease with which you can then produce each issue. Your masthead will stay the same each time. Other standard features, such as a table of contents (if the publication is long enough to warrant one), the column layout, etc. will remain the same with every issue. You simply have to write the articles and insert them.

Your newsletter can be as simple as one sheet of paper, folded in thirds, with one panel left blank for the address label and your bulk mail indicia. Or you can do an 11" x 17" folded in half to form an 8-1/2" x 11" four-page newsletter. You can add pages in this manner to come up with 8, 12, or 16 pages. Of course, you have to be a pretty prolific writer to come up with that much news on a regular basis.

A newsletter can be an excellent contact method for your bookstores, wholesalers, and readers alike. Start small and let it grow.

What doesn't work

We mentioned that our poll of fiction publishers pointed out some marketing strategies that don't work. These were (again in no particular order):

Direct mail to individuals
Radio
Paid advertising
Mail order
Trade show displays

Although to some degree, we have used all of these with some success, let's look at some caveats.

Direct mail to individuals

A pre-publication notice of the impending release of your new book can certainly work well to draw some orders from friends and family members. Especially if you can time the mailing to one of the major gift-giving times of year (Christmas or Spring), and if you are willing to offer a "friends and family" discount, you'll surely get some orders.

It is fine to do this. Just realize that you'll never sell out your entire print run this way and it certainly can't be the only marketing strategy you have in your bag of tricks.

We have done mailings to memberships of various writing groups. While these have generated some orders, and have certainly helped with the author name recognition within the organization, these mailings have not really paid for themselves. We get far more queries from hopeful authors who want us to look at their manuscripts than we get orders for books. Better to get your name recognition from the free publicity you'll get by using your Keylist contacts.

Radio

Our respondents to this particular poll did not say whether they were referring to radio advertising or radio interviews. As previously discussed, radio interviews can certainly be rewarding, especially if you can do them the day before or the day of a signing in a local store.

Radio advertising is not often done for books, especially fiction, even by the largest publishers. As expensive as radio air time is, I can't imagine this being a good investment of your advertising dollars.

Paid advertising

Again, as we discussed in the previous section, paid advertising should only be considered in areas where you know you will reach a very specific market. An ad in *Publisher's Weekly* or the *New York Times* will almost certainly never pay for itself. While many non-fiction titles lend themselves to a small classified ad where the reader will send away for the book by mail, this almost never happens with fiction and would probably be a waste of money.

Stick with smaller genre-specific publications and budget your advertising dollars carefully.

Mail order

Mail order to individuals is probably much like running a classified ad. Not many people buy fiction this way. You are better off targeting your mail order campaigns toward bookstores and libraries, then generating enthusiasm among readers in other ways. See the next chapter on making a name for yourself as an author for more ideas along these lines.

Trade show displays

If you are a one or two book publisher and you plan to rent a booth at the big American Booksellers Association convention, travel to the convention city, stay in a hotel for a week, and sell lots of books—don't. You can never make a trip of this kind pay off with just a couple of titles.

TIP: Make the most of trade show exposure by following up afterward—the sooner the better.

Use the services of a trade show exhibitor like International Titles, or take advantage of using low-cost shared space with one of the publisher's organizations like PMA or SPAN. Most trade show exhibitors will provide you with a listing of everyone who stopped by the booth during the show. At the very least you should get a list of any inquiries about your book(s). You must, must follow up with these leads yourself. Don't expect to get lots of direct sales from the show. More on trade shows in Chapter 9 on subsidiary rights.

Chapter 8

Making a Name for Yourself as an Author

In Chapter 1, we suggested strongly that you work to define your novel in terms of genre. In addition to defining your book, it is much easier to make a name for yourself as an author within a specific field.

Join writer's organizations within your genre. Check the Appendix for the addresses if you have not already done so. Add their newsletter editors' names to your Keylist and mail them regular notices of your booksignings and speaking engagements. If you have a TV or radio interview, tell them. If you had an article published, tell them. Get your name in each newsletter's Member News column as often as possible. It sounds like a small thing, but people remember names they hear or read often.

An old marketing truism is called the Rule of 7. It takes seven repetitions for people to remember your product. In this case, you are the product.

Staging a Pre-publication party

Only the biggest authors at the big publishing houses get a party in their honor, a pre-publication gala. After all the hard work you've done to get your book written, designed, and printed, you deserve a party too. One of our authors actually had three of them—one for their friends and business associates, one for the entire neighborhood (the setting for the book), and one for members of the writing group she belongs to.

You can make the party as large or small as you wish, a picnic or a real black-tie gala. Hold it at home, at a bookstore, or rent the ballroom at a fancy hotel—whatever your budget and lifestyle dictate.

This is your time to shine. Your friends, relatives, and associates have known you were working on a book for a long time. Let it make an auspicious debut. Recruit a friend to handle the money end of things, or work with a local bookstore. Sometimes you can get them to send someone to your choice of locale to handle sales, while you sign books and socialize.

Invite the book editor of your local paper to attend. If they can't actually send anyone to the party, you should send them a press release and photo afterward.

Be creative in designing your announcements. One of our authors made up oversized postcards announcing the "birth" of the book at 1lb. 4oz. The reverse of this card was a color picture of the book cover.

Author Tours

At big publishing houses, the top name authors get sent on author tours. You'll notice, when you read the Forecasts section (the book reviews) in the back of *Publisher's Weekly*, that the tour will be mentioned as a way of letting booksellers know that this book is getting extra attention.

Well, you are the biggest author at your publishing house, and you can arrange your own author tour. And you don't have to spend thousands on airfare and hotels. You can keep it fairly simple and relatively inexpensive.

Start where you live. No matter how small a town, you can start your tour at home. My town is tiny, population 600, with

Secret's Shadow
An Oak Park Mystery
by psychotherapist Alex Matthews, LCSW

Cass is faced with a therapist's worst nightmare: a client suicide, lapsed insurance, and a note blaming the therapy. And to make matters worse, a homeless cat moves into her house; the client's brother insists she join his investigation; and attempts are made on her life.

Relentless in forcing each family member to give up their secret, Cass finally confronts the one person whose shadow envelops them all.

Alex Matthews, MSW
546 N Humphrey Ave
Oak Park, IL 60302

ADDRESS CORRECTION REQUESTED

Alex & Allen Matthews
proudly announce the birth of
a book

Secret's Shadow

born April, 1996   1 lbs 4oz

Dear friend,

As an unknown, first-time mystery author, Alex has to hit the book-sign-presentation-promo trail. If you can spare the time to attend one of her talks (free admission and, please, no obligation to buy), we would greatly appreciate it.

If you can't attend but would like a signed copy, call one of the stores and request that a book be held for you. Secret's Shadow can also be ordered directly from Intrigue Press.

Allen

The Characters That Inhabit Your Mind
Presentation at 2:00 PM
Book Signing at 3:00 PM

May 4, 1996
Centuries & Sleuths
(708) 848-7243
743 Garfield
Oak Park

June 6, 1996
Borders Books & Music
(708) 574-0800
Route 83 & 16th Street
Oakbrook

Intrigue Press - Angel Fire New Mexico - (800) 996-9783

Author's announcement of debut novel

no book store. But two different gift shops carry my books and they both love to sponsor booksignings.

Decide how much time you have. Can you take a week or two off to hit the road? Or do you need to confine your travels to weekends?

Get out the road map. How far can you go in a comfortable day's drive? Even if you can only be away on weekends, you can go north one time, south the next, east, then west. Plot out some towns you can get to within a half day or so.

Check the yellow pages (available at the library if you don't have copies of them) and find the bookstores in those towns. Make some calls. Try to line up one signing for Saturday afternoon and another for Sunday. The booksellers would probably prefer that you don't do two appearances in the same town within a day of each other, so try to find two different towns along your route that can accommodate you. Or do one bookstore and one library appearance.

With weekend trips like this, you can cover a 400 or 500 mile radius of your home city, with minimal expense for travel and only one or two overnight stays per trip.

If you can get away for a week or two, you can use a progressive travel technique. Decide roughly which direction you'd like to travel. Perhaps you have friends or relatives in a city two states away and you'd like to set that as your goal.

Now look at all the points in between. Try to pick towns that are approximately a day's drive, whatever is comfortable for you. Again, find some bookstores and make some calls. Tell them you are an author, describe your book a little if they haven't already heard of it, and tell them you'll be in their city on (whatever date). Would they be willing to do a signing?

You'll get turned down sometimes. It's expensive and time-consuming for stores to sponsor booksignings. Some of them do many signings, others hardly ever do. If they aren't interested, be gracious, thank them, tell them you'd be glad to stop by the store and sign whatever books they might have in stock, or just to meet them. Keep calling other stores in the area until you get a 'yes' answer. Put them on your calendar.

Now, starting at that town, plot out another comfortable day's drive. See where you would end up and call stores in this town. See how it works?

If you can't get a signing in a store, try the library in the town you're visiting. See if you can give a short talk or reading, and tell them you'd be willing to bring books that the attendees can purchase and have signed.

If you have a children's book, schools are another excellent opportunity. You normally can't sell books at a school, but combine one or two speaking engagements in the afternoon with a store signing that evening and you'll dramatically increase attendance at the signing. Give each student a bookmark or pen and they'll manage to get Mom and Dad to the bookstore for you.

Back at your road map, continue a day at a time until you reach your destination. Try to plot a different route on the way home so you'll pass through different towns coming back. You have just planned an author tour.

TIP: Where do you sign a book? On the title page, in the blank space between the book title and the author name.

Making the most of the tour

If you do some preliminary work before you ever get into the car, your tour can be much more profitable. Here's how.

You can get lots of free press for your tour if you play your cards right. Get the names and addresses of the newspapers, radio and TV stations in each town where you'll be signing. You need to do this at least a couple of weeks before the tour starts.

Newspapers

Send a press release about your book. The one you used in the beginning to announce your book to the stores will work, but you'll want to personalize it for each of the towns you'll be visiting. If you have any personal connection in any of these places, be sure to mention it. Did you ever live there? Work there? Have a relative who lived (or still lives) there? Does your day-job company have a branch office there? Mention anything.

If you can't come up with any personal connection, at least mention the date, place and time of your booksigning. If you've planned to talk about writing or do a reading from your book, mention those. Somehow, an author speaking to a group (libraries and schools are great for this) is more newsworthy than someone merely selling books.

So, make your press release as newsworthy as you can. Include an extra book cover or dust jacket and one of your author photos. If the newspaper has a book review column, send them a book and request that they review it the week of your signing.

You can make professional press kits, just like the big guys do. Get some dual pocket portfolio folders. The glossy ones are nice. Pick a color that goes well with your book cover. Now take one of your spare dust jackets or covers and cut off the back and flaps so that you have just the front cover. Glue this to the front of the folder.

Inside, put your press release and author photo into the pocket on the right hand side. On the left side, include copies of any good reviews you've received, pasted up with the header of the publication. Be sure to include ordering information about the book. Tell what local stores it is available in and additionally list your publisher phone number.

FOR RELEASE JANUARY 15, 1996   Contact: Lee Ellison

                                                   505-377-3474

Former Denver Resident

Announces Debut Novel

Imagine what could happen if foreign terrorists gained access to America's nuclear power. Imagine their being able to hold hostage a U.S. Navy nuclear-powered aircraft carrier, with all its weaponry, nuclear reactors, aircraft, and a crew of over 5,000 men. Imagine the carrier sailing into New York Harbor with the terrorists ready to initiate a nuclear incident.

Author Dan Shelton, formerly of Denver, has done just that in his new suspense espionage novel, *Assault on the Venture*. Drawing upon his own experience as an aviation ordnanceman in the Navy, Shelton has created a vivid cast of characters and an utterly terrifying, utterly believable situation. Fans of Tom Clancy and Robert Ludlum will find Shelton's story readable, his characters human, and his plot full of devious twists.

Shelton lived in Denver in the 1960s and '70s, piloting the Flight For Life helicopters on several thousand rescue flights. He also worked for a time at Sundstrand Corp. and played professional guitar at local night spots. Shelton now operates his own helicopter service in northern New Mexico where he resides with his wife, mystery author Connie Shelton.

Assault on the Venture is available in hardcover for $21.95 at these area bookstores:

_____, _____, _____.

or by calling 1-800-996-9783 to order by credit card.

# # #

Press release tailored to locale

Home-Owned   Home-Operated

THE SUNDAY JOURNAL

115th Year, No. 183 ■ 226 Pages in 22 Sections   Sunday Morning, July 2, 1995   ■ Copyright© 1995, Journal Publishing Co. $1 ■ Made in USA ★★★★

'Gamble' an impressive debut mystery

"Deadly Gamble"
By Connie Shelton
Intrigue Press, $21.95, 211 pp.

Review by Steve Brewer

Self-published books always are a little suspect, but Angel Fire resident Connie Shelton's Intrigue Press has created a quality product in "Deadly Gamble," the first of a new mystery series featuring Albuquerque accountant Charlie Parker.

Not only is the hardcover book nicely appointed, but the story's an upbeat little charmer that will be of particular interest to people who recognize the sights and sounds of Albuquerque.

Charlie (short for Charlotte) Parker works with her brother in a private investigations firm. Usually, Ron does the surveillance and Charlie keeps the books. But Ron's out of town when an old friend, Stacy North, suddenly appears in the office, begging for Charlie's help. Stacy's had a fling with a low-life she met at Tanoan Country Club and he stole her Rolex watch. Stacy's got to get the watch back before her abusive husband Brad

finds out. For added interest, Brad is Charlie's former boyfriend, stolen away by Stacy years earlier.

Unable to turn down an old (if estranged) friend in need, Charlie tracks down the hocked watch and solves the problem. But then the low-life, Gary Detweiller, is found murdered. It doesn't take the police long to find the Stacy connection (though how they do is never spelled out) and Charlie's soon trying to help her friend beat a murder rap.

Shelton has a chatty, breezy style, though she could give us a little less of what Charlie eats and the boring paperwork that makes up her usual, non-detecting life. But New Mexicans can forgive a little distraction in exchange for site-specific revelations about the Duke City.

Journal staff writer Steve Brewer is the author of "Baby Face," which was published last month.

■ ■ ■

Angel Fire author Connie Shelton signs copies of "Deadly Gamble" 2-4 p.m. Saturday at Borders Books & Music in Winrock Center.

Reviews with Masthead from Newspaper

Introducing the second Charlie Parker mystery, coming October, 1995 from Intrigue Press.

We are now taking prepublication orders for the second in this exciting series.

Vacations Can Be Murder
by Connie Shelton

ISBN 0-9643161-1-0
LCCN 95-77210
216 pages, Hardcover, $21.95

Order from Intrigue Press
P.O. Box 456
Angel Fire, NM 87710
or through major wholesalers
Baker & Taylor, Ingram, Brodart, etc.

Here's what the critics said about the first Charlie Parker mystery:

"This is a well-plotted debut mystery with a nice surprise ending and some excellent characterizations. Charlie, in particular, is slick, appealing, and nobody's fool -- just what readers want in an amateur sleuth. Look forward to the next installment in what shapes up to be a promising series." -- *Booklist, January 15, 1995*

"This is a dandy. Don't miss it!" -- *Book Talk, March, 1995*

"An impressive debut mystery." -- *The Albuquerque Journal*

"Pacing is excellent, cover intriguing (so necessary to move the books off the shelf)..."
-- *Dottie Ambler, The Tattered Cover Bookstore*

"Shelton has created a female sleuth with an original slant to her methods. The mystery itself was in question until the very end. It's a fun and fast read." -- *Small Press Magazine*

"Very impressed with the professionalism shown in the production of this exciting mystery." -- *Books of the Southwest, Tucson, Arizona*

"...a light, fun read... an interesting mix of characters and relationships ... a cut above most first efforts." -- *Bloodhound, The Crime Writer's Connection*

"Congratulations to both author Shelton and Intrigue Press on this wonderful introduction to both talent centers." -- *Book Talk*

"Charlie Parker has a heart as big as all outdoors and it almost spells her finale in *Deadly Gamble*. Connie Shelton's debut mystery offers a down-home view of Albuquerque and a charming new PI."
-- *Carolyn G. Hart, author of the Death on Demand and Henrie O. mysteries.*

Example of review for press kit

TIP: To dissipate nervous energy or stop hands from shaking before an interview, press the palms of your hands together firmly for 5 seconds, then release.

Radio

Radio stations are required, as part of being granted their FCC license, to run a certain amount of public service programming. If your visit to their town can be classified in any way to be a public service, you might just get some free air time.

Send a public service announcement (PSA) if your author appearance includes a free-to-the-public speaking event, such as at a library, bookstore, or for a class of school kids. Again, personalize the PSA for each town you will visit.

PSAs must follow some guidelines if you want them to be used. Air time is doled out and every second accounted for. So, you must fit the criteria. Your PSA should be an exact 15 or 30 seconds in length when read aloud. Write it out and then practice reading it aloud and timing it. You'll be surprised — 15 seconds is really a very few words. You'll have to choose them carefully.

The other way to get some coverage on the radio is with a live interview. These are usually done over the phone and can be done from your home or your hotel room if you are on the road at the time. As we mentioned earlier, it's usually the non-fiction authors who get invited for radio interviews, but there are a few ways you can increase your odds.

Develop a sheet of interview questions. As a good friend who retired from broadcast journalism once told me, "Media people are extremely lazy. The more of their job you do for them, the better coverage you'll get." (He said it, not I.)

Anyway, think of any newsworthy angle your book might have. Make up some questions along those lines. Some general

FOR IMMEDIATE RELEASE   October 1, 1995

Please run the week of October 1-7, 1995

15 second Public Service Annoucement

New Mexico author Connie Shelton will speak at the main branch of the Albuquerque
Public Library at 423 Central NW, Friday evening at 7:00. Shelton will read from her new
mystery novel, *Vacations Can Be Murder*, and give a short talk on mystery writing. A
question and answer period will follow. The event is free to the public.

Sample PSA

For Immediate Release:
Contact: Lee Ellison, 505-377-3474

Interview Questions for
Connie Shelton

➻ Your first mystery, *Deadly Gamble*, was published in February of this year. But we understand that you have actually written six books?

➻ Your sleuth is a woman named Charlie Parker, who lives in Albuquerque. How did you choose Charlie's name and how did you pick Albuquerque for your location?

➻ What type of readers would Charlie appeal to?

➻ It says here on the back cover of your book that you wanted to grow up to be Nancy Drew. Explain that.

➻ Where do you get your ideas? Do you do a lot of research?

➻ A good mystery is like a complicated puzzle. How do you figure out the plot of the crime? Do you write an outline first? Do you start at the beginning, middle or end of the story?

➻ Albuquerque has a lot of writers of all types. Is there something about New Mexico that attracts creative people? How did you get started?

➻ What advice could you give someone who wants to write a novel?

➻ What would be the first thing an aspiring writer should do?

➻ What about breaking into the publishing game? Isn't it difficult?

➻ Charlie Parker is the lead character in a series. When will the next book be out?

➻ And the second Charlie Parker mystery takes place in Hawaii? How did you happen to choose that location?

➻ How many more Charlie Parker books can we look forward to?

➻ Where are your books available locally?

Sample Interview Questions

questions about how you came to write the book, how you chose your genre, your location, etc, can also be interesting. Come up with 10-15 questions and print them out on a sheet of your publisher stationery.

Send the press kit and interview questions in advance, then follow up with a phone call. The interviewer will want to coordinate a time for the two of you to connect if the interview will be done over the phone. If it's a studio interview, they will tell you what time to be there.

Television

Getting any real TV time is tougher, because not too many talk shows feature fiction authors. But it can be worth contacting them. One of the local stations in our state does a noon news broadcast, during which the host works in very quick live interviews with a wide variety of people. I appeared there to plug my first book the day before a signing, wedged between Karl Malone, the basketball star, and the Humane Society's adoptable pet of the week.

No prep work or rehearsal was involved. I had contacted the station about a month before the scheduled booksigning, and the host called to tell me what time to be at the station with my book in hand. At air time, he walked in, introduced himself to all the guests, and set my book on the news desk facing the camera.

Between news segments, the program director shuffled guests in and out of the guest chair. When my segment came, the host was ready with about three quick questions about the book and plot. He ended by reiterating the date, place and time of the signing and it was all over in about three minutes flat. He carried it all—I only had to talk to him and avoid thinking about the camera (ha!). It's a good thing, because my heart was pounding wildly the whole time.

The whole episode was short and easy, and it did result in

several people coming to the signing specifically because they saw me on TV. It was certainly worth doing.

When you do a TV or radio spot like this, it's a good idea to leave a card with the receptionist on your way out of the station. Take a 3x5" card and write out the title of the book, your name, the bookstore and time of the signing. Frequently, people who only caught part of the broadcast will call the station to get the details. Make sure the person who answers the phone can supply them.

Your own contacts

In addition to getting as much press as possible, you can draw more people to the signing with personal contacts. Look in the membership directories of the writer's organizations you belong to. If you have the names on your database, it's a simple matter to sort them out by zip codes for the towns you will visit and print mailing labels of the names and addresses.

Make up postcards introducing yourself as a fellow member of the group. By this time they've seen your name in their newsletter several times and they know who you are and are anxious to meet you, right? Give the details of the signing and a personal plea about how much it would mean to you if they could come. Send cards also to any relatives or old friends who live nearby, too.

Okay, you've done all your preliminary contacts and you're ready to hit the road. If this is a weekend jaunt, call each of the bookstores a few days before you leave, just to be sure they received the books they ordered in advance and that the schedule is still on. Always carry extra books in the car with you, just in case.

If you are doing the full-blown two week tour, you should confirm with each store a few days before you are due there. And if you are really with it, you might fax a second press release to each of the radio stations along the way. One author we know faxed her interview questions to the radio station in the next town so she would have an interview lined up as soon as she arrived. Her husband traveled with her, which is a real help, and he took care of the publicity end of things while she played "star."

What the bookstore does

Generally, the store who is sponsoring your signing will do some advertising of the event. But don't expect much if you aren't a name author. If the store sends a newsletter to its regular customers, they usually use this means of letting people know about visiting authors. They may place a small ad in the book section of the local paper the week before your appearance.

If you have color postcards of your book, extra flyers, bookmarks (which you can easily make yourself), or some of those great ballpoint pens, send them to the store ahead of time. They will hand them out to customers for a week or two before the event to help draw more people.

The signing itself might turn out to be just about anything. Some stores, particularly small ones where the owner is always there, will make an event of it, serving wine and cheese or snacks. In other places, you get a chair and a table with a few copies of your book on it. One time, I signed alongside a Pulitzer Prize winner. Needless to say, her table was swarmed, while I felt lucky to sell three books. Sometimes it just works out that way.

Anything you can do to identify yourself as an author will help. Believe it or not, sometimes customers walk past your table and stare, trying to figure out who you are and why you are sitting there. You can wear a name tag "Joe Smith, Author." You can make a small easel-type poster with some wording such as "Joe Smith, author of the new thriller, *Kill 'em Dead*, here today." Use your book cover to decorate the poster. Stand it beside you on the table.

Above all, whether the turnout is great or lousy, or some-where in between, be friendly and gracious to everyone who comes by. If absolutely no one shows up, as happened to a friend of mine, you can still use the time well. Chat with the bookstore employees and put them at ease (they are probably just as embarrassed by this as you are). Tell them a little about your book, enough to make them want to read it. These are the people who are on the front line with the readers every day. Your very best friend may turn out to be the bookstore employee who absolutely loves your book. In many instances, the majority of a book's sales happen after the actual signing, so don't lose heart even if the turnout isn't great.

TIP: Always send a thank you note to the store after a signing.

Building bookseller enthusiasm

Without a doubt, one of the key ways in which many "small" books have made it to best seller status is through the enthusiasm of booksellers. The rise of *Bridges of Madison County* through handselling is legendary. The bad news is that booksellers have access to thousands of titles to recom-mend to their customers. The good news is that, generally, people in the book business are here because they love books, they love to read, and they love to share their enthusiasm.

Sending advance reading copies of your book to selected stores, visiting stores whenever you can, and keeping stores updated when you get good reviews are all good ways to get them to read and recommend your book.

Getting speaking engagements

There's something about being published. You may have been writing for years, working to perfect your craft, and yet, until you are published, you're just a wannabe. Anyway, that seems to be the perception. Once you are a published author, people suddenly want you. Give a talk or appear on a panel, and soon you begin getting invitations for more talks and panels.

Attending conferences is fun, in whatever capacity you go, but you'll sell far more books if you get the chance to speak. So how do you get into this chain of popularity?

First off, if this sounds like a good marketing opportunity, but you are terrified of speaking, work on overcoming that fear. Join Toastmasters or take a public speaking course. Attend a few genre conferences as a fan to take some of the fear out of it.

Check out the conferences or fan conventions you might want to attend. Listings of upcoming events should be announced in your genre fan magazines or writer's newsletters. If you are able to sign up far enough in advance, simply inquire about the possibility of being included on a panel or giving a talk.

Different conferences follow different formats. Some are geared toward writers and are meant to include instructional workshops. They will normally feature multiple tracks, with individual speakers presenting different topics. This is where your expertise in a particular area will shine.

Evaluate your strong points. What is it about your writing that seems to get mentioned most often? Are your characters praised for being witty or vulnerable or courageous? Do you have a character or setting that stands out or a plot that somehow transcends the genre? In other words, what could beginning writers learn from you? Mention these to the programming organizer, along with any awards you have won or other outstanding achievements you have attained.

Many genre or fan conferences are planned with a much more casual format. Rather than instructional programming, the sessions are often panel discussions. Four or five authors with something in common will kick around ideas, give background information about their books, and in general let their fans get to know them. After the panel discussion, there will usually be booksigning time. The fans flock to the book dealer's room to get books by those authors they liked the sounds of, then stand in line to get the books signed. With any luck you won't get seated next to Mary Higgins Clark, whose signing line will stretch out the door.

In determining presenters for either the instructional or the informal format, the conference organizers can go many directions. Many times they will ask for input from those authors interested in participating. It's not enough to say, "I'd like to be a speaker," you've got to give them an idea what you can do. Sometimes they will want a written proposal.

You might want to attend a conference or two as research before you volunteer to speak. Or you can jump right in. If you can get your hands on the program for the same event from the previous year, it will give you a good idea what they are looking for. Look at the topics presented last year. Chances are, they will use the same format, but they will want to cover different topics with different people. Get creative and try to fill in the gaps. If possible, talk to the person in charge of programming and let them know a bit about yourself and your book. An idea may spring forth as the conversation progresses.

Be flexible. If you write sensuous romances, it's fine to speak on that topic. But after about three panels on the subject, you need to change your slant or risk becoming stale. Can you approach another romance topic? Can you discuss women in jeopardy or some other aspect of the genre? It's tough to get pigeon-holed into giving the very same presentation over and over until finally no one wants you because "it's been done."

Once you're there

Conference etiquette is not that different from plain good manners anywhere. Be personable and polite. Be friendly when people approach you. Graciously give autographs when asked (refrain from giggling with joy.)

There are authors who, once they've become a "name," take on a star attitude. They resent being approached by anyone lesser. They have a circle of people, other big name authors, with whom they will chat but anyone else gets frozen out. They have lots of fans who've read their books, but once those fans meet said star, they become disillusioned with the real personality and the brilliant writing loses its shine.

Plenty of big star authors are genuinely nice people, and their fans and colleagues know and love them.

Take the hint. Your attitude can kill your career.

Networking

Networking opportunities abound at conferences. It might be tempting to attend your panel then scoot to your room to get some more writing done. After all, we writers are accustomed to solitary hours at our computers. But you've paid good money to be at this conference—use the time wisely.

As we mentioned earlier, getting to know the booksellers present is one of the best moves you can make. Meeting other authors can yield some wonderful benefits, too. We picked up the lead that led us to a four-book audio contract in a casual fifteen minute conversation with another author. Future speaking engagements have been spawned during a chat in the hallway.

Attend the planned social gatherings. Join a table where you don't know anyone. A typical banquet table might seat eight or ten people. That's eight or ten book sales if you are friendly and genuinely nice.

Hang out where the rest of the conference attendees are hanging out. You don't have to become a barfly if that's not your inclination. Go where you feel comfortable. Don't put on the high sales pressure everywhere you go, just be yourself.

Becoming Collectible

It varies by genre, but I know mystery is this way and I believe sci-fi and westerns also enjoy this phenomenon—modern books becoming collectible.

When an author has published several titles and has become known, there is frequently a demand for some of his/her first titles and suddenly this author (or sometimes it's just a particular title) has become collectible. Those who follow the genre closely will begin buying up copies and driving the prices up.

I used to read a book once, then pass it along to a friend or donate it to the library. When I learned that a first edition of Sue Grafton's mystery *"A" is for Alibi* now sells somewhere in the range of $850, I decided to hang on to my old books a bit longer.

What creates a modern collectible? Format, size of print run, and having the author's signature are among the features collectors look for.

Hardcover or paperback? Most of the experts agree that they are more likely to find hardcovers when shopping used bookstores and flea markets. Mainly because those books are more durable. It's rare for a paperback to survive intact very long, although if they do, they too can increase dramatically in value.

The experts also say that, given a choice, they prefer to collect hardcovers.

Signed or not? Signed. Definitely. Whenever possible, they try to attend author signings. Should a signed copy be personalized? That's a big question. Many true collectors prefer to buy copies with only the author's signature. However, if the book is for a private collection and the person doesn't have any plans of selling, it's fun to have the author inscribe the book with the recipient's name. Sometimes a book inscribed with the date is more valuable, for instance, if signed on its original publication date or at a particular event. When signing books, it's always a good idea to ask the buyer if he or she wants it personally inscribed, or if they'd rather have signature only.

First printings are always the most desirable, especially if the first print run was a small one. The market may later be saturated with mass market paperback copies of that title, but the original (particularly hardcover) will almost assuredly go up.

Most experts also say that books, like art, are a speculative investment and they first buy what they like. And collectors don't necessarily rummage around garages and flea markets. Many of the brand-new books in stores today will someday become collectible.

What's a hypermodern? This term is being thrown around more and more nowadays as increasingly new titles gain collectability. According to the experts, some titles have reached the $100 to $200 price range as soon as a year or two after publication. An original copy of John Grisham's *A Time to Kill* reportedly is priced in the $3,500 range.

Advice to publishers and authors? Hold on to some of those first editions of your own book.

50 Quick and Cheap Promotion Ideas

1. Insert postcards into each book, soliciting comments from your readers.

2. Have your promotional efforts in place before the books hit the shelves. Timing is crucial.

3. Have your photo taken at book signings for later use in

press kits and newspaper articles.

4. Develop a gimmick at conferences and speaking engagements. Hold a drawing or contest for a small gift. One mystery author gives away bottles of "Blood Red" wine. A romance author uses heart-shaped earrings.

5. Take a guest book to all your signings to accumulate more names for your mailing list.

6. Have "Author Autographed" stickers made up. Put them on books you've signed for a store's stock.

7. Have color postcards made of your book cover. On the reverse, print favorable reviews or leave space to list your booksigning dates and places. Put one in every piece of mail that leaves the house, leave them with bookstores, mail them to members of your writer's organization.

8. Keep your local bookstores supplied with press releases, bookmarks, flyers, and stickers.

9. Answer all fan mail. Send fans a pen or other little gift.

10. Offer to be a speaker for civic or business groups.

11. Get poster-sized color copies made of your book cover (inexpensive at copy shops). Leave space at the bottom to write in dates and times of signings. Send posters to stores in advance of signing.

12. Get T-shirts made with book cover art. Wear shirt to signings and conferences.

13. Make up your own questions for TV and radio interviews. Give personal info that ties into the book theme. Mention the title of your book often during the interview.

14. Take extra promotion materials to conferences, such as bookmarks, postcards, flyers. Put them on the giveaway table.

15. Send pens ahead to conference organizers to put in attendees' registration packets.

16. Photocopy the first chapter of your book and send to stores in advance as a teaser.

17. Use an eye-catching author photo. Make it fun, some-

thing that reflects your personality and your book.

18. Send press releases to newspapers in the towns you plan to visit. Make your book and yourself interesting. Include an extra book cover. Tie it in with a signing or appearance.

19. Network with other authors. Plan signings together.

20. Look for ways to tie your book in to local events. Point out these tie-ins to get on radio and TV talk shows.

21. Use props at your booksigning table—a centerpiece, costume, or table cloth that ties in with your book.

22. Make a small easel to set on your booksigning table. Include your author photo, one of your book covers, and quotes from favorable reviews.

23. Pass out novelty items at booksignings or speaking engagements—pens, toys, bookmarks, bumper stickers, some tie-in to the book's theme, i.e., a recipe.

24. Offer to bring snacks, wine and cheese, cookies and punch, etc. if store doesn't plan to do them.

25. Have a drawing for a prize—lunch with author, a book, t-shirt, or book bag.

26. Donate a book to a charity or library benefit auction. Or better yet, offer to use the winning bidder's name as a character in your next book.

27. Hold a signing at an unusual place—a winery, theater, restaurant.

28. Time your mailings to readers and stores to coincide with the spring Mother's Day, Graduation, Father's Day season. Suggest books as ideal gifts. (This is the second biggest gift season of the year.)

29. Collect business cards at conferences and add the names to your mailing list.

30. Nominate your book for awards. Enter your work in contests.

31. Save programs from conferences where you are a speaker. Get extras if possible to use in future publicity.

32. Attend bookseller and librarian conventions. Ask if you

can do a reading or short talk.

33. Ask friends and relatives to order your book through stores rather than from you, if they don't mind. Stores remember those authors whose names come up often. If the store doesn't have the book in stock, have your friend ask them to order it.

34. Get to know your local bookstore owner well. Buy books from them. Send them updates on your activities.

35. Get your author photo reproduced inexpensively at a photo lab. Use them generously with press kits and bookstores.

36. Send thank you notes after a signing or appearance. Send holiday cards to your press contacts and bookstores where you've signed.

37. Make your own bookmarks very inexpensively. Using your computer and laser printer, lay them out five or six to a page. Include a scan or photocopy of your book cover. Print them on card stock (65# bond), then cut them apart.

38. Make extra special bookmarks, decorated in an imaginative way. For her *Writers of the Purple Sage*, Barbara Burnett Smith glued small pieces of purple sage plant to each bookmark.

39. Stop in at every bookstore you pass and ask if they have your book in stock. (If they ordered through wholesalers, you might not know.) Offer to autograph stock books. If they don't have the book, show them a copy and leave ordering information with them.

40. Get bookplates, autograph them, and send to stores that you are unable to visit.

41. Have friends request your book at their library.

42. Include your author photo with publicity materials you send to stores.

43. Introduce yourself to booksellers at conferences. Chances are, they've come from all over the country. Now they'll remember you and carry word about your books back

home with them.

44. Carry the vital information about your book with you. The ISBN, cover price, ordering information, etc. should be printed on something you can leave with any store or library you visit.

45. Make up a sheet of your best reviews or a montage of newspaper clippings. Use it generously in mailings, visits to stores, anyplace you need to get the word out.

46. Don't improvise a speech—it shows. Write down some notes and practice your talk aloud.

47. Don't write a word-for-word speech and read it. Boring!

48. Prepare your handouts and visual aids for a speech well in advance. Have them at your fingertips so you won't fumble around looking for them.

49. Persist!

50. Believe in yourself!

51. (This is a freebie idea.) Get a copy of John Kremer's *1001 Ways to Market Your Books*

Chapter 9

Subsidiary Rights

Just as the large trade publishers seek subsidiary rights for their titles, so can you. What do we mean by sub rights? Mass market paperback, foreign language reprints, audio, film, TV. Basically, any other form that your book can take. We'll touch briefly on some methods for seeking these potentially lucrative rights.

Mass market paperback

Especially if you've published your book in hardcover, the next natural step is to release a paperback version. That's normally what the big guys do, roughly a year after the original hardcover release.

You can publish mass market titles yourself. We know of several small presses who have done it. But, because of the larger print runs required and the completely different marketing strategy (especially if you want to get the books into supermarkets, airports, and discount chains) it makes sense to look for a trade publisher to handle the mass market version.

How to approach them?

Basically the same way you would with a manuscript, except that now you have more ammunition. Get the names of publishing houses from *Writer's Market* or *LMP*. Find out the name of the editor who handles your type of book. You may have met some at conferences, and it certainly makes sense to take advantage of these contacts.

Send a copy of your book, along with a query letter. Be sure to quote any good reviews you've gotten. They'll also want to know how your sales have gone. If your first print run sold out, even if it wasn't a huge one, that's important. Let them know what you, as an author, are doing to promote your book. Your press kit, with clippings of any newspaper articles, reviews, speaking appearances, can be included for some extra punch.

As with any submission, follow up after some time has gone by, and keep trying.

Foreign language rights

We've had a number of inquiries about foreign language rights for our titles. Foreign markets can often be even more lucrative than U.S. publication rights, so they are definitely worth pursuing.

You can research the names of publishers and approach them in the same way you would an American publisher. We've also had good success with exhibiting our books at foreign book fairs. The big ones are in Paris, Frankfurt, London, Madrid, Tokyo, and Taipei.

You can see tens of thousands of dollars in travel and trade show expenses flying out the window, right? Actually, we've exhibited at each of these places for $100 or less per title.

TIP: Make the most of trade shows by sending follow-up materials afterward. The exhibit service will usually provide a list of interested buyers after the show.

Publisher organizations such as PMA and SPAN, and book exhibition services such as International Titles offer trade show exhibit opportunities at very reasonable rates. They also exhibit at the American Booksellers Association and American Library Association annual conventions here in the U.S.

They rent the booth space, travel to the convention, man the booth during show hours, talk with buyers visiting the show, and furnish you with a list of sales leads afterward. All for a fee of somewhere between $60 and $100 per title. Not bad.

Afterward, you can follow up with the buyers overseas by fax or by mail, send them books if they requested them, and make your own deals. Don't expect orders for books from a foreign trade show—that's not what they are about. These are usually buyers from publishing houses or distributors in other countries who are interested in publishing American titles.

What you get for your money with co-op trade show exhibits can vary with who is handling it, so be sure to ask questions and read their information carefully. We've used International Titles on several occasions and are very happy with the job they do.

To get the most out of trade shows, you must do your part, too. It's up to you to provide an incentive for attendees to buy your book. Make up a half sheet of your best reviews. Most foreign buyers are familiar with American publications like *PW, Library Journal, Booklist*, and *Kirkus*, so reviews from those publications will carry weight with them. Copy the review sheet onto eye-catching colored paper. Glue this to the inside flyleaf of the display copy of your book. If your cover art is distinctive enough to make a buyer pick up the book (it is, isn't it?), they'll flip it open and read your best reviews. Also, be sure to take advantage of any other promotion you can do. At some shows, the exhibitor will only want one display copy of your book. At others, you can also send flyers or catalogs. Be sure you include complete ordering information, including your wholesalers and distributors, with these materials.

Audio

We mentioned that we signed a four-book audio deal for our Charlie Parker mysteries. Approach audio publishers in much the same way you do with a trade book publisher. Send a copy of the book and some idea of what you've done to promote yourself.

Different publishers have different needs. The one we signed with happens to specialize in mysteries and westerns because that fits with their marketing plans. And since their markets do not include many mystery bookstores, we negotiated a deep discount so we can purchase tapes, sell them at the store's standard discount rate, and still make money. Do some research and you can find out who publishes your type of work.

Another possibility is to record your own audio tapes. Many of the same reasons might apply as for publishing your own books—retaining control, marketing, etc. Since abridging a book for its audio version is a very common practice, that alone might make you opt for doing your own. At least any cuts made will be of your own choosing.

There are companies who will help with this, much as your book printer does your books. They can furnish professional talent to record the book, make the master tapes, duplicate as many copies as you want, and even design and produce the packaging. We've not worked with an audio packager, but you can shop around, get bids, learn about them before committing any money. See the Appendix for a listing of some audio producers.

Film or television rights

Along with mass-market paperback rights, film and television rights are among the most lucrative sub rights you might sell. Option prices can range from as little as $500 to as much as $100,000. $10,000 is about average. With an option, the producer is buying the exclusive rights to a book for a specified period of time (usually 90 days to 1 year), while they look for financing for the project. If, by the time the option period is over, they have not exercised their option, or picked it up, it expires and you are free to seek another producer. You also get to keep the money from the original option. Many properties are optioned that are never actually produced, but the money can still be very good.

If the producer does exercise the option, the purchase price might go for anywhere from $25,000 to $2.5 million. Some well-known authors, such as John Grisham, have also negotiated for a percentage of the movie's gross.

Certain books lend themselves well to film, others to TV, and some don't work for adaptations at all. Be realistic when assessing your chances at making it to film. Is your story one of an internal journey made by the main character, a dilemma that is mostly verbalized? Or is it a story full of action, adventure, romance? In other words, is it visual? Can you picture it on the screen?

Now think about the types of stories you see in each format. Some plots work better on television, others in the movies. For instance, our action adventure novel, *Assault on the Venture*, is an espionage thriller that takes place aboard an aircraft carrier, which is in the process of circumnavigating the globe. We were thrilled when a Hollywood agent requested the book for a client. Later, we were disappointed to learn that the client was considering it for a TV movie and decided that *Assault* would be too high-budget with all its explosions and exotic locations, not to mention the use of an aircraft carrier with 5,000 men aboard. Now we're in the process of sending it out to feature film producers.

Carolyn Hart's mystery, *Dead Man's Island*, was picked

as a made-for-TV movie starring Barbara Eden and William Shatner. And, of course, Larry McMurtry's western *Lonesome Dove* has hit legendary status as a mini-series.

Anyway, you get the idea. The book must fit a producer's needs, so think about it and target those production companies that are likely to use your type of story. Send them a short pitch letter. It has to be vivid and snappy and convince them in three or four pages that this is the greatest story they've ever heard. It has to be different from other movies that have been done, but familiar enough that they feel the concept is tried and true.

That's the good news. The tough part is breaking in. Unless you live in southern California or have contacts in the film industry, you'll find it difficult to do. Most rights sales are made through literary agents or scouts who specialize in this field. Look in *Literary Market Place* for listings or check the other publications listed in the Appendix. We've also listed a few of the top agencies. If you live in a state that is very active in the film industry, as New Mexico is, you may want to look for a literary agent near you. The advantage is that you will be able to meet them and establish a relationship. The disadvantage is that they are not in Hollywood and may not have their foot in the door quite as far as an agent who is near the industry.

Chapter 10

Selling Out to the Big Guys

Getting a trade publisher to buy your book is very much like approaching them to buy paperback or other reprint rights. The first step is to find those publishers who publish your type of work. With genre fiction, you probably already have a pretty good idea of who they are. Again, if you've met some editors from these large houses at conferences, start with them. Don't, however, query just one publishing house at a time. As you know from your earlier days, if you submitted manuscripts to many publishers, it takes them months to get back to you. The process of contacting a dozen publishers can take a couple of years this way. This time, use the mud-on-the-wall approach. Throw a lot out there and see what sticks.

Once you have collected the names of the appropriate acquisitions editors at all the publishing houses that publish your genre, work on an irresistible query letter. Open with a paragraph that will catch their attention. Tell them something about your sales of the book. If you went into a second or third printing, by all means, brag about it. Tell them what marketing efforts you have made. If your book has sold in the tens of thousands with nothing more than word of mouth advertising, they will begin to visualize the great things it could do with some of their advertising clout behind it. Be truthful. Sales figures in this industry are not secret, and they can find out if the major wholesalers like Baker & Taylor or Ingram have moved lots of copies.

Tell them something about yourself. Express your ability to tour and to speak before audiences. List your speaking credentials at conferences. Tell them exactly which readers the book will appeal to. Include copies of all the good reviews you received for the book, along with any of your marketing materials, press coverage, etc. Offer them an examination copy of the book if they would like to be considered as a reprint publisher for this title, or send review copies along with the query letter. Use a phrase such as, "We are currently seeking bids for reprint rights on this book," to let them know that you are contacting multiple publishers.

With any luck, you should get positive responses from more than one house. For this reason and out of pure caution, you should never agree to any deal over the phone. If you've had one phone call with a potential offer, your first step should be to contact all the other publishers you queried who have not already rejected the book.

Call each and speak to the editor to whom you addressed the letter. Ask if your materials have been received and mention the positive reactions you've had from other publishers. Inquire as to whether the publishing house might need additional information. This may pique their interest or it may just speed the rejection letter to you, but at least you know where you stand with them. You won't have accepted a deal with one publisher while other interested parties may still be out there.

If you do receive offers from more than one publishing house, you can set up a *rights auction*. Some books have received as many as nine out of ten positive responses. In this case, it will be in your best interest to get them bidding against each other.

To hold an auction, set the closing date for the bids, set the rules for the auction, and a minimum bid which will be accepted. If one bidder will guarantee this minimum bid, you may offer this amount to them as the *floor*. In exchange, this bidder is usually offered a *topping privilege,* meaning that they have the right to top the highest bid at the end by 10% or whatever you have agreed upon.

Bidders may submit written bids by the closing date, or you may choose to take telephone bids on the closing date. Once you have all the bids, review them carefully. Call the lower bidders and see if they want to top the highest bid. Continue doing this until all the bidders have dropped out, then sell the reprint rights to the highest bidder. If one of the bidders has a topping privilege, call them last to see if they wish to exercise this privilege.

Now that you've successfully sold the rights, it will be time to review the contract they offer and start negotiating the best terms you can get for yourself. Here are some preliminary questions you should ask:

- How many copies do they plan to print?
- What would the cover price be?
- How much would they budget for marketing? (For hard-covers, this should be somewhere around $1 per book. 20,000 copies equals $20,000.)
- How long do they anticipate the book would stay in print?
- What royalty percentage are they offering? You can find the current standard rates in *Writer's Market* on a standard sale of an untried manuscript. Since your book has a proven track record, point that out and try to negotiate a better rate.
- Are royalties based on the cover price or the discounted (net) price? It's to your advantage to have the rate calculated on the cover price.

You will probably be offered an advance against royalties, payable half upon signing and half upon acceptance of the finished and revised manuscript. Sometimes the payout is 1/3 on signing, 1/3 on receipt of manuscript, and 1/3 on publication. Take into account how much time and work, not to mention money, you've put into the publishing and marketing of your book. You've put forth the effort to bring this book to market, and you deserve more than the standard new-author advance. Keep in mind, too, that selling to a trade publisher may well mean that you can no longer sell your self published version. If you do not negotiate for a high enough advance, there goes your steady income until the book earns out its advance and starts generating royalties.

On the matter of whether or not you can continue to sell your self-published books, this can be another negotiating point in the contract. If you have established markets outside the regular bookstore and library markets, try to retain those for yourself. Be sure you can still sell books at speaking engagements and appearances. If your own version of the book will no longer be available, at least be sure you can purchase copies from the publisher at a deep discount — 60% or more.

Another very important point to cover in the contract is the matter of the publication date. Make them stipulate that the book will be published within a year of signing the contract. Otherwise, they can stall and take forever to get the book to market. You'll be stuck with only part of the advance.

Seek the return of all rights if the book goes out of print. Try also to retain all other rights except the primary ones you are selling with this contract: North American English language rights. Keep mail order, electronic, audio, video and any others for yourself. Essentially, review every paragraph of the contract and try to make it as favorable to yourself as possible. You can bet the trade publisher will start with a contract that is very much in his favor.

Use good sense and good negotiating skills in working out the details. You can blow the whole deal by being too hard-nosed about certain points. Realize that a contract negotiation should be a win/win situation for both sides. Be willing to give in on small points in exchange for holding on to items that are important to you. If you feel nervous about negotiating a contract, you might study some books on negotiating skills. Or you can have an agent step in to negotiate the contract once you have a ready buyer. You'll have to give up a percentage, but they may be able to get you enough extra money that it will be worth your while.

Chapter 11

Getting Help

What happens when you simply can't do it all? Taking on the entire responsibility for running a business does mean a lot of work. You may get tired of trying to handle it all. You may find certain tasks that you don't enjoy as well as others. Your talents or interests may not encompass all that is required of you.

Don't despair and certainly don't give up. There are several jobs you can farm out without necessarily causing your company to grow too quickly. Just remember that every job you can do yourself saves money that will otherwise have to be paid out to someone else, cutting into your bottom line. With that in mind, here are some jobs that can easily be turned over to others.

TIP: Expand your business slowly and with a plan. Rapid expansion harms more often than it helps.

Publicity

Publicists are readily available to handle many of the arrangements for your radio, television, and book tour appearances. Many of them work on a commission basis, charging only for the appearances they book for you, plus expenses. Others charge a retainer fee, a monthly fee, or some other arrangement. They can take on as much or as little of the work as you wish them to, from making press kits, to mailing reading copies of your books to stores, to phoning or faxing the talk show circuit to arrange speaking engagements for you.

Ask lots of questions. Most publicists, like publishers, have their specialized areas of expertise. If you write science fiction, a publicist who specializes in cookbooks is not likely to know how to handle your books. You would not be doing either yourself or your publicist a favor by signing on with them.

Find someone with experience in your genre. Ask exactly what they will do for you and exactly what it will cost. Talk to other authors or publishers who have worked with this publicist to find out if they were happy with the experience.

To find a publicist, check the Appendix in this book, *Literary Market Place*, or advertisements in publishing newsletters.

Order fulfillment

If you live someplace where it is impossible to warehouse your own books, or if you find yourself simply too busy for the billing and shipping of orders, you might want to take advantage of a fulfillment service.

Most will warehouse the books, and offer invoicing, shipping, handling of returns and credits. Some will collect money from your accounts and then send you monthly statements of account activity.

In our case, most of our sales are in case lots to wholesalers or bookstores. Fulfillment is not a great time consumer, but if you do many one-book sales, such as direct to consumers through mail order, it can take a lot of time to fill those orders every day.

You can find fulfillment companies listed in *LMP*, or in the advertising sections of such publications as *Publisher's Weekly* or the PMA newsletter. Many book printers also offer fulfillment services, which makes the warehousing solution easy. The books don't have to be shipped to you first.

Again, ask questions. There will probably be a storage fee for the books. You'll pay postage costs on all books shipped, plus a handling fee per book. Find out if you are also expected to pay for insurance to protect your books against fire or flood while in the warehouse, and if there are any other fees.

Agents

If you decide to pursue foreign, reprint, or film rights for your books, you may want to turn this over to a literary agent. You may find it somewhat easier to get an agent once you are published, especially if you are actively involved in writer's conferences. This is how I found my agent, or perhaps she found me. At any rate, we were able to talk and get to know each other, and we've had a very amiable relationship ever since, as she works to secure subsidiary rights for our books.

In looking for an agent, check first through those contacts you've made through your writing over the years. Perhaps an agent you met or contacted several years ago would now be interested in looking at your books. Send them a book and a query letter. Let them know how your sales have been going, and be sure to include good reviews you've gotten.

If you don't have any ready-made contacts, pursue other avenues. Ask other authors or small publishers for recommendations. Look in *LMP* or *Writer's Market*. Agents, too, tend to specialize by genre or fiction vs. non-fiction. Do your homework and find someone who will take a genuine interest in representing your type of book.

Accounting and taxes

Face it, many creative people just can't handle numbers. If the task of producing financial reports for your business is just too intimidating, you need an accountant or bookkeeper. Having accurate financial data is too crucial to ignore, so don't just let it slide.

There are many computerized accounting programs today that will do much of the work. Especially if you use your computer to do your order entry, much of the information you need will already be there. The software we use is interactive, meaning that when an order is invoiced, the computer automatically subtracts the merchandise from inventory and charges the dollar amount to the customer's account. At month's end, it prints statements of account for the customers and income statements and balance sheets for us.

It is critical that you know where you stand money-wise. If you simply cannot handle the paperwork, look around for someone who can. Perhaps your spouse can do it. Or maybe you'll need to look for a bookkeeper. You can avoid adding an employee to the payroll by finding a bookkeeping service that will produce financial statements and charge you by the month.

At least quarterly it is a good idea to have an accountant review your financial statements from a tax standpoint. The accountant can advise you if you need to be making estimated quarterly tax payments and if you are on track tax-wise for the end of the year.

There are numerous small jobs you can farm out without having to put employees on the payroll, increasing your taxes and paperwork responsibilities. The tax laws can be complex, so you will want to consult with your accountant to find out what fits your situation. The IRS defines an employee, whose wages are subject to social security and Medicare taxes, as one where all of the following apply:

1. The service contract states or implies that almost all of the services are to be performed personally by the individual.

2. The individual has little or no investment in the equipment and property used to perform the services (other than

an investment in transportation facilities.)

3. The individual performs services for you on a continuing basis.

If you pay an individual $600 or more in a year, you need to issue them a form 1099-MISC at the end of the year.

If you buy services from another business, such as the graphics firm that does your cover art, your publicist, etc., be sure you get an itemized invoice for services rendered and file that invoice with your paid bills. These kinds of people are not your employees because they are working in their own place at their own speed and are simply billing you for services rendered.

You can get your own kids to help. Cleaning the office, emptying trash, wrapping packages, and stuffing envelopes are tasks that many youngsters can handle. They'll learn a sense of responsibility and feel like they are earning their allowance. If you make it into the big leagues and the big tax brackets, you can even divert some of that income to your kids by paying them a reasonable amount for the work they do. There are some good books on running a small business and the tax considerations involved listed in the Appendix. Send for *Publication 334, Tax Guide for Small Business* by calling the Internal Revenue Service at 1-800-TAX-FORM. It is a valuable source for answers to many small business questions.

Publishing Other Authors

Once the word gets out that there is a new publishing house specializing in your genre, you'll begin to get query letters from other authors, wondering if you might be interested in publishing their books. After all, they don't realize that you started out to publish only your own. You've heard editors from trade publishers talk about how many manuscripts they receive, but you just don't realize how many hungry authors are out there looking for a publisher until their work starts to cross your desk.

We resisted at first, not sure if we were willing to put our money on someone else's book. Gradually, I began reading some of the work that came to me, and found that, while much of it really is mediocre, there is some excellent writing out there. Many of these authors don't want to get involved with New York houses because of the hassles they've heard about. Others have tried and made no headway. Your decision, of course, is whether you want to be a one-book (or one-author) house, or whether you wish to expand.

There are severals ways to look at this:

Against—
- You hardly have time to do your own writing, publishing, and promoting as it is.
- Where will the money come from?
- You really don't care about promoting any other authors.

For—
- The other authors will do the writing and much of the promoting, actually freeing up more of your time.
- Unless you need to draw income from your publishing company to live on, the profit from one title can be reinvested into production costs for the next title. (*Most small businesses have to reinvest all profits back into the business for the first few years.*)
- By having more than one author, your publishing house suddenly becomes bigger in many people's minds than just a self-publishing operation.

These are some of the initial considerations, and you may have your own as well. You will need to formulate your own policies regarding submissions from other authors. Here are some suggestions that may help when making your decisions.

Stay within your genre. You have spent months developing your contacts, your databases, your marketing strategy. Do you really want to start all over in a whole new field? It would be much smarter to stay with what you know and work new titles into your existing marketing plans.

Be sure that any new authors will make a committment to promoting their own work. As a publisher, you will still need to target mailings to bookstores, get review copies into the right hands, and advertise to readers, but the book will sell much, much better if the author is also out there working hard. Authors need to commit to setting up their own signings, attending fan conventions, developing and informing their own Keylists. Look for writers who are already active in writing organizations and who understand (or are willing to learn about) how publishing and promotion work.

We prefer to look for authors who have a second book already written and more in the works. As you know by now, an author spends much time on promotion in the first year of publication. If that second book is already written, it is easy to get it into the market before enthusiasm for the first book has cooled. Our theory is that we want to build a career for every author, to publish a series of books and achieve momentum. You can't do that with a one-book author.

Have a contract. This item should have probably been listed first because it is crucial. Any time you have financial dealings with someone, you need to get everything in writing. There is a book contract template in the book *Business & Legal Forms for Authors & Self-Publishers* by Tad Crawford, available through Writer's Digest Books. This contract is a very author-slanted version. We also obtained a copy of a book contract used by a big publishing house that was very publisher-slanted. We developed our author contract to be a balance between the two, wanting to be fair to our authors and to ourselves.

Our contract gives the author a small advance against

royalties and a royalty comparable with other small presses listed in *Writer's Market.*

Another way to go might be to work a co-publishing arrangement with authors you would like to publish. The upside is that they can help bear the cost. The downside is that you will gain the reputation of being a subsidy publisher, and we all know how they get treated. Our attitude was that, even though we could not offer a large advance, it was not worth tainting our reputation to take an author's money.

Once you've made the decision to take on other authors, you need to set some guidelines, for yourself and for the submissions you'll accept.

How many books per year can you feasibly take on? Think about your situation. Are you doing everything yourself? Do you have help, or are you ready to take on the commitment of employees? In our case, we decided that we could manage two books a year if we had to write them ourselves, as many as four if we had other authors. So we set our policy—we publish 2-4 titles per year.

Develop a guidelines letter that will tell writers what you are looking for. Put it in your computer so you can print it out any time. Be sure to cover such topics as:

What genre do you publish? If you publish romances, but don't especially care for historicals, tell them. There is no point in having writers send things that you know you won't buy.

How long should the book be? Most publishers express this in terms of word count. Give an average range so you won't be inundated with novelettes of 20,000 words or gigantic tomes of 100,000 plus. If the standards within your genre are usually 70,000 to 90,000 words, tell them that's what you want.

Tell them how many titles you publish per year.

Tell them how much promotion effort you expect the author to make.

You don't have to commit to an advance or royalty amount at this point. You can simply say that these vary with each contract. This gives you the freedom to negotiate.

Be honest about your publishing timetable. If you only publish two books per year and you already have commitments for four titles, then your list is full for the coming two years. Remember, a contract is a commitment for both parties. Don't take on more than you can realistically do.

Unless you want to be absolutely swamped with reading material, don't get a listing in *Writer's Market* or *LMP*. We have never listed our publishing company anywhere, and we receive 40-50 submissions a year. Considering that we can publish a maximum of four books a year (one of which will be my own), that's about fifteen times more than we could possibly buy. Naturally, only a small percentage of these will be of interest, but it still takes time to read them and send rejection letters.

Having been on the receiving end of a few form rejection letters in my time, I wanted to offer suggestions where possible on those books I turned down. Amazingly, I found that some writers would argue with me, while others wanted to start an on-going discussion of their work. I'm sorry, but I just don't have the time, and I'm beginning to see why the form rejection is so widely used. Use your own judgement on how to handle this.

Publishing another author's work can be fulfilling in the sense that you know you are helping someone else to achieve their dream. And you never know, you just might discover the next John Grisham.

Chapter 12

The Non-Commercial Book

Certain books, no matter how much work you put into them and how dearly you love them, are not considered commercial books. Family histories, very localized history books, literary anthologies, and small collections of poetry might be among these. That's not to say that they don't deserve to be published—they do, by all means.

Rather than going through all the work of getting set up with wholesalers and worrying about subsidiary rights and such, your life can be much simpler. Let's talk a little about each of these types of books, then look at some of the considerations when publishing them.

Family Histories

As our population continues to age, many of us in the baby boomer generation realize our own mortality, and want to investigate and preserve our parent's and grandparent's stories. The recent book, *To Our Children's Children*, went into mega-sales after the authors appeared on *Oprah* to talk about the process of getting those stories written or recorded. The techniques of taking oral histories are now taught in college. Clearly, we are a population yearning to know about our past.

With the aid of one of these interview guides, you may have

already collected mounds of data and interviews from an elderly relative and now you would like to see it published in book form. Or you might like to write your own life story to pass along to your children and grandchildren. Whether to do a straight transcription of interview tapes or to write the story in narrative form so it reads like a story is your decision. Now you just need to know how to get it into book form.

Localized history books

In the same way, perhaps, that we are increasingly interested in our family histories, many of us live in places with a past, and we would like to research and write that history. Whether it be a city, a small town, a mountain valley, or even a two-block neighborhood within a city, you've unearthed some fascinating facts and would now like to get them into book form.

You may have taken oral histories from old-timers in the area; you may have scoured every library for a hundred miles; you may have visited cemeteries, museums and historic sites. However you collected the data, now that you've written the story, you want to see it published.

Literary anthologies and poetry

While there are certainly anthologies and poetry books out there with commercial potential, some are done mainly for fun or for the enjoyment and sharing of those whose work is included. This is not to belittle the quality of the work. You simply might not want to go to the marketing efforts required to get this book out nationwide. Perhaps you only want enough copies for friends and family.

By publishing these types of books yourself, you have the freedom to be more creative with both your interior and exterior format. In addressing all the abovementioned types of books, there are a couple of crucial questions you need to ask yourself early on.

How limited is your sales potential? Your grandmother's life story, particularly if published as a straight transcript from taped interviews, might only appeal to the members of your own family. Including extended aunts, uncles and cousins, that might be 100 people or so. If the history of your neighborhood sells three copies to every person who lives there, it might still be fewer than 200 books. There is no reason to consider a print run of 5,000 copies, no matter how reasonable the cost per copy.

So, the first step is to realistically try to assess how many books to print. Yes, the cost per book will be less as you print more copies, but you may not want to store an extra thousand books in your garage for the rest of your life. There are book printers who specialize in short run jobs and can print as few as 50 or 100 books. Look in the Appendix for listings.

What format would you like to publish? Not bound by conventions of genre and the fight for bookstore shelf space, you can do pretty much what you want—within your budget— hard cover, soft cover, saddle stitched. Think, too, about the interior. Grandma's story might deserve an extra heavy cream paper. Perhaps your local history will include photos. Maybe you have some terrific pen and ink drawings to enhance that anthology. All these factors will come into consideration when getting bids from printers.

As with any other book, you'll need to figure out your specifications. Review Chapter Four on Design and Production to determine size, format, and number of pages. Decide on your cover design. Will you do a hardcover with gold stamping for the title? Will you want a dust jacket or not? Maybe softcover is what you had in mind. Will you use one color, two-color, or four-color process for the cover?

Now, look in the Appendix or check references such as *LMP* for book printers that specialize in short print runs. If you intend to print a very few copies, this may determine which printer you will use. Some have lower minimums than others. Try to find at least two or three companies to get bids from. It's extra work to solicit bids, but can save you hundreds or even thousands of dollars.

Work out your specifications using the tips in Chapter Four and mail or fax it to the printers. Ask each printing company to also send you a sample book made with roughly the same specs you are requesting. This will give you the chance to see the quality of their work and some idea of what your finished book might look like. Within a few days to a week or two, you should have some choices. Look them over carefully. The prices might vary widely, and so might the quality of the sample books. The cheapest printer might not be the best choice. At least, by getting several bids, you have the opportunity to make an informed choice.

Covering your costs

Many times, with a non-commercial book, you are publishing it as a non-profit venture. However, non-profit doesn't have to mean "loss" financially. In many cases, simply covering costs with maybe a little to spare, is the goal.

For example, maybe your writer's group wants to publish an anthology of the members' work. Your cost will be $3.50 per book for 500 copies (this is only an example), for a total of $1,750. With freight, your total cost might be $1,850. This is assuming you volunteer your typesetting time and get the cover art donated as well. You have 20 contributors to the book and they each commit to purchase 20 copies of the book at $4.50 each. That's 400 books sold — $1,800 right there. If each of the 20 contributors will also agree to put names of their friends and family on a club mailing list, you can mail out a flyer to generate more sales. Of course these would be at a suggested retail price, perhaps $6 to $10 per book. Make it a price that will seem reasonable to the consumer. Since you won't be discounting to wholesalers and bookstores, these books are allowed to break the 5-8 times markup rule.

If you are publishing a local history book (and this idea will work for the above-mentioned anthology as well), look for donations or pre-sell the books. For instance, how about approaching your Chamber of Commerce with your idea of writing a history of the area. They may want to either donate some money toward the project in exchange for a mention on the back cover or acknowledgements page, or they might even want to purchase books, especially if they can get them at cost. This is a win-win situation. Here's how it works.

Ask them to examine their budget and determine how much they can contribute to the project. Meanwhile, you will figure out the size and format of the book so you'll have some idea of production costs. Let's say they decide they can give you $3,000 toward the book. You've figured out that you can print 1,000 books for $4,500. You still need to come up with $1,500. You can either approach another business or non-profit organization to help foot the rest of the bill, or simply divide the production run proportionally with your sponsor. In the above example, the Chamber of Commerce has contributed 2/3 of the production cost ($3,000 out of the $4,500 needed) so they get 2/3 of the finished books, or roughly 660. They will probably sell them through their office or their member businesses, so they win. You win because you still have 340 books to sell at retail price to bookstores, libraries, personal contacts and any other sources you can think of.

This approach works well with businesses and professionals, too. Banks, insurance companies, and other businesses are always interested in giveaways for their customers. You can make any arrangement that is mutually beneficial as to cost and number of copies they get for their money. Some of them are willing to donate the money, especially to a non-profit writer's group, in exchange for a mention like, "This book is made possible through the generosity of First National Bank." You still have all the books to sell and the bank gets free advertising with every one that goes out.

With a family history, the approach might be slightly different, unless Uncle Herb who wrote the book just happens to be rich enough and kindly enough to pay for the printing and just give the books away. And that might be exactly the case. If not, though, you can still recoup the cost of printing.

Offer the books to family members and old friends of the family at cost. Several years ago, one of my great-uncles wrote a book telling of his and his siblings early life. I had always adored this uncle and had not heard many of those old stories, so I didn't quibble a bit at paying $12 for a copy. Of course, now knowing what I do about publishing, I know the book could have been produced for less money, but that usually isn't the point with a family book; it's the information contained and the memento factor. He has since passed away, at the age of 93, and I'm so glad to have a copy of his book.

There are many ways you can sell these books without much out-of-pocket expense. Word of mouth tends to run strong in families. Tell Grandma—she'll get the word out. Make it quick and easy for people to order the book. Make up a flyer with a short order form at the bottom. Pick a few key points from the book to give it some sales appeal. Make the order form simple and state the price of the book, including postage, clearly. People should just be able to fill in their name and address and write a check. The easier you make it, the more you'll sell.

With the help of other family members, put together a family mailing list, or use your Christmas card list or personal mailing list. If you have a large family, postage can be expensive, so combine this mailing with another occasion, such as notification of the next family reunion, your annual holiday letter, or whatever.

Other possible customers for a family memoir might in-

Voices from the Valley

The Moreno Valley Writer's Guild

is pleased to announce publication of its second annual anthology.

Voices from the Valley, Volume II

features several award winning authors. Including works by:

- Leslie Lenz
- Pamela Barnes Brennaman
- Elaine V. Sandberg-Jarzen
- Claude McDonald
- Thomas Hardy Potter
- Paul Casper
- Connie Shelton
- Dan Shelton
- Kathy Schafer
- Phoenix Helm Simpson
- Don N. Nation
- Georganne Adams Lenham
- F.R. Gualda
- Anita Pendleton
- Mary Vonder Hoya
- Frances D. Palleson
- Buster Kirk
- Vicki Jameson
- Clyde Herring

Also, still available if you missed it the first time — Voices from the Valley, Volume I, including works by these fine authors:

- Margaret Cottingham • Don N. Nation • Vickie Jameson • Mary Ollerich • Claude McDonald
- Anita Pendleton • Deborah Halpern • Connie Shelton • Georganne Adams • Pamela Barnes
- Scott Miller • Mary Vonder Hoya • Mary Anne Wheeler • Audrey Anne Elizabeth Bucks
- Paul Casper

Yes, I would like to order *Voices from the Valley*. I enclose my check payable to Moreno Valley Writer's Guild.

Ship to:

Name _____

_____ Volume I at $4.50 each = _____
_____ Volume II at $5.50 each = _____
SAVE!! Order both for only $9.00 _____
Shipping (see rates below) =   _____
Total   _____

Address _____

City, ST, Zip _____

Shipping: 1 book $1.50, 2 books $2.50,
3 or more books, $3.00 plus $.50 per additional book

Mail to: Moreno Valley Writer's Guild, PO Box 416, Angel Fire, NM 87710

Combined Flyer and Order Form

clude residents of the town where the author grew up or members of their church. You might send a press release or place a small classified ad in the hometown paper, especially if it is a small town. Give the price of the book and your address where they should mail a check. Place a notice in the church bulletin.

An advantage of a personal memoir book is that you can pre-sell the books before you go to press. Send out the above-mentioned announcements and advertisements first. Give people a deadline by which to order and an approximate date when you will ship the finished books. See what kind of response you get. You may think that Grandma's story will only sell 50 copies or so, but you might get orders for 100 or more. It will be more cost effective to print 100 or 150 to start with than to do two or three press runs of 50 each, because you underestimated. On the other hand, grandiose ideas of Grandma's popularity might have led you to print 1,000 copies before you realized that you'd only get orders for 100.

Whether you decide to do a family book, a history book, poetry, or an anthology for profit or just for the joy of publishing, it can be a valuable experience and you never know where it might lead. You still have the option of presenting the book to stores or trade publishers for additional sales.

Conclusion

The Juggling Act

Managing your time so you can be a writer, publisher, marketer, shipping clerk, and still have time for your family and friends can be a real trick.

A motivational speaker recently told me, "Time is the one thing that we are all given the same amount of. How we choose to use our time is what makes the difference." It's true, we all have twenty-four hours in each day, seven days in each week, 365 days in each year. So, why do some people seem to accomplish so much while others have a hard time finishing one task in a day? And when you think about it, aren't these usually the people who always seem to complain, "I just didn't have time to get that done this week."

So how do we stretch our hours to find our peak productivity? There are probably many answers to that, and there are some excellent books on the market on time management. Here are some tips from the experts.

1. Stay healthy. Nothing slows you down more than feeling physically sluggish. Eat right, exercise moderately, avoid excess drink and smoking, take your vitamins, and get enough sleep.

2. Be aware of time-wasters.

Television is probably the biggest. If you routinely sit in front of the tube from 6:00 to 10:00 every evening, that's 28 hours a week (not counting weekends, when the sports channels run all day.)

Procrastination is an insidious one. Get the tasks you don't enjoy done first and it's amazing how quickly the rest of the work (the things you like to do) will get accomplished.

The telephone is another time waster. If you are on deadline for a book, there is nothing that will get you off track faster than a call from a friend who just wants to chat. By the time the chat is over, an hour later, you've completely lost your train of thought. Let the answering machine catch the calls, go somewhere away from phones, just do whatever it takes to stay on track.

3. Get organized. With very few exceptions, most people cannot work well in the middle of a mess. If your desk is piled high with files, your bookshelf overflows, and little scraps of paper float around the office, you can't possibly work efficiently.

Buy a file cabinet if you don't already have one. Get some hanging file folders with labels and start making files for all that stuff that tends to get piled up. If you already have files but can never seem to find anything, go through them. Are the files properly marked for easy identification of the contents? It is easier to find the information you want if you label the file with its primary content. For instance, MARKETING IDEAS is easier to locate when you are thinking about how to sell your book, than a file entitled IDEAS—MARKETING. Because you might also have IDEAS—NEW AUTHORS, IDEAS—BOOKSTORES, IDEAS—NEXT BOOK.

One fairly quick way to start a filing system is to gather up all the items you plan to file. Start sorting them into stacks on the table or the floor. Put everything of similar type into a stack, like financial information, sales information, marketing information, wholesaler/distributor information. Once you have everything delegated to a stack somewhere, look at the individual stacks. How can you break them down into reasonable file sizes?

Your financial stack may include your business plan (you did do one back in Chapter 2, didn't you?), your bank statements, your merchant credit card information, invoices to your customers, and your financial statements from month to month (whether you generate these yourself with your accounting software or have an accountant to them). Take each of these items and group them with their own kind. Make a separate file for each and hang the files in the cabinet.

Go to the next stack and do the same. When you have all the files done, look at them. If a file contains only one or two pieces of paper, you might not really need a separate file for that category. Could those items be combined with some similar ones? If you have a file that is already overflowing, perhaps you need to consider breaking down its contents into more categories for ease of locating the information. You decide. The goal is to have enough files, but not too many, so that the information is easy to find. A top-notch organized person should be able to put his/her hands on any given piece of paper in the entire office within three minutes. If you routinely spend more time than this looking for things, you need to get more organized.

If you perform work for more than one business or entity, set aside separate file space for each. Don't intermingle files in the same drawer. Make a separate drawer for your volunteer activities or your speaking engagements.

4. Write everything down. *Everything!* Don't trust anything to memory, from meeting dates, to publicity ideas, to watering the plants. Keep a calendar on your desk, one of those with a separate page for each day (or a notebook-style day planner if that's more your style) and write down every deadline, every meeting, every letter or follow-up call you need to make.

5. Group your work tasks. Look at your in-basket. What do you have to accomplish today? Four orders have come in the mail, there are three phone calls to return and a dozen

letters to write. Then you have that new flyer you want to design. Among these typical tasks, there is probably one you love to do and one you hate to do and some others you feel neutral about.

First, sort the tasks into groups. There is nothing more inefficient than just grabbing from the top of the stack. If you make one phone call, then write one letter, then invoice an order, then make another phone call, you can easily spend the entire day without getting through your stack. Today's incoming mail will bring another stack and in less than a week, you'll be hopelessly behind. Sort the big stack into little ones. Think in terms of your computer software's capabilities. Which tasks will be done on the word processor — the letters, the flyer. Which tasks will be done through accounting — the order entry, perhaps balancing the bank statement.

Now, you can approach the small stacks in a couple of ways. I like to start the day in a positive way, so I enter my incoming orders first. That's money coming into the company and that's a good feeling. Some people like to get the most unpleasant task out of the way first so they can enjoy the rest of the day. Some would rather save the most unpleasant task for last (this is probably most of us). That's fine, but don't let yourself start putting the most unpleasant task off to the next day, then the next, etc. Those letters or those collections calls, or whatever it is you don't like doing still have to get done and it will catch up with you one day.

Within your various tasks, try to group similar ones together. For instance, if you bill all your orders, then type all the shipping labels, then carry all the invoices to your warehouse (garage or wherever), pull all the books and package them, then write them all up in your UPS shipper book, it is much more efficient than following all these steps for one order, then starting over at the beginning with the second order, and the third, and so on.

If you are writing letters, you may find that you can save

lots of time by doing similar ones together. You may want to send queries to ten foreign publishers about subsidiary rights for your new book. You will be saying essentially the same thing to all of them, so use your word processor to its fullest advantage. Compose the text of the letter, then simply change the address header and perhaps a sentence or two to personalize it to each. The first letter may take a little time, but the subsequent ones will zip through. You will have finished ten letters in little more time than one would normally take.

Try to use this kind of logic when planning your projects. Don't waste time on one query letter when you can send ten, don't write or call one delinquent account if you have several. Batch your work into similar tasks and get them all done at once.

And finally, build balance into your life. Working, playing, learning, and spirituality all have important places in everyone's life. Excluding any of them leads to imbalance and stress. And stress saps your energy and enthusiasm.

In conclusion, I have to say that starting my own publishing business has been one of the most fun, exciting, busy, and fulfilling times of my life. As with anything worth doing, it's been a lot of work, but it has been enjoyable work.

Study your craft, do your market research, ask questions of suppliers. Educate yourself, as you would with any new business you plan to invest in. Here is a timetable you can follow to get your project going and keep it on track.

We wish you all the best with your publishing venture.

Who Comes First? What Comes Second?

Doing this project in an orderly fashion

Assuming that you've examined your motivations for publishing, be they commercial, non-profit, or merely ego-boosting, you will have decided whether or not to form a business entity for your publishing venture. This guide assumes that you will want to establish a publishing business and strive for commercial success. These steps will lead you through that process. It is strongly suggested that you read this entire book once before proceeding and that you seek outside help in areas you do not fully understand. Those publishing non-commercial books will obviously not follow every step outlined here; figure out which parts pertain to your project.

FIRST—*Setting up your business—8-9 months or more before pub date*

1. Read this book completely. Refer back to sections of interest and take notes or highlight entries. Read other business guides or consult an attorney to determine the form you want to use for your business: sole-proprietorship, partnership, LLC, LLP, or corporation. (If you choose partnership, LLC, LLP or corporation, have the papers drawn up.)

2. Subscribe to *Publisher's Weekly* and get a copy of *Literary Market Place*.

3. Choose your publishing company name and research to be sure it is not already in use.

4. Get a post office box and open a business checking account.

5. Contact Bowker for ABI info and apply for ISBN numbers and log sheet.

6. File a fictitious name statement if required in your area.

7. Contact the IRS for form SS-4 to obtain an Employer Identification Number (required even if you have no employees) unless you are a sole proprietor.

8. Contact your state department of Taxation for a tax ID number.

9. Contact your city clerk's office to find out about local business licensing requirements. Be sure there are no restrictions against home offices in your area.

10. Call the phone company for a business line. Request an 800 or 888 toll-free number if you plan to solicit mail orders.

11. Have stationery, envelopes and business cards printed.

12. Write the Library of Congress to get LCCN forms.

13. Contact prominent authors requesting they read your book and give blurbs.

SECOND—*When your book is written—7-8 months before pub date*

1. Research your title to see if it has been used.

2. Get signed permissions for any copyrighted material you may be using, such as quotes from songs, books, cartoons.

3. Have an editor or book doctor edit the manuscript.

4. Make corrections on manuscript.

5. In your word processor or layout program, set up your book design and save it as a style sheet or format. Transfer a few pages of manuscript text into the format to check margins and typeface.

6. Prepare a cast-off to determine book length. Remember to add front and back matter to your total page count.

7. Submit your specifications to several book printers for quotes.

8. Get author photo taken.

9. Contact cover designer and start work on cover.

10. When quotes arrive from printers, determine which you will use, then use our formula for determining cover price.

11. Assign an ISBN. Order a Bookland EAN scanning symbol. Complete the LCCN form.

12. Complete the ABI form for Bowker. Send new title information to Baker & Taylor, Ingram, other wholesalers and distributors.

13. Typeset your book, transferring it from your word processing program to your layout program. Assign styles to all headers, footers, chapter headings, etc. Double check pagination for errors. Print out a copy of the entire book.

14. Photocopy the entire book (galleys) and send to prime reviewers as "Uncorrected Proofs." Send copies to prominent authors for blurbs.

15. Write text for jacket or cover. Send it to cover artist.

16. Contact your KEYLIST with the exciting news that your book is being published and the pub date.

THIRD—*Going to press—6-7 months before pub date*

1. Proofread typeset pages and have someone else who has never seen the book proof them also. Mark corrections and make them on computer.

2. Get cover art proof from artist, discuss any changes and have them made.

Send author photo and EAN scanning symbol to artist.

3. Contact book clubs and appropriate serial rights buyers to interest them in subsidiary rights.

4. Prepare your marketing plan. Write news release, sales letter, mock-up review, reviewer's request form. Decide which stores will get complimentary advance reading copies of your book.

5. Do a final review/proofing of the typeset pages, including all front and back matter. Make a photocopy of the typeset pages for your file and mail the originals to the printer.

FOURTH — *The Waiting Game—5-6 months before pub date*

1. Develop your mailing lists. Get names of reviewers, newsletters, bookstores, libraries, wholesalers, media sources, etc. Look especially for those who specialize in your genre. Enter names you find on your own into your data base, or rent lists from mailing list services.

2. Make up a personal mailing list which includes names of friends, relatives, business associates, membership organizations, neighbors — essentially everyone who knows your name. Enter these into your personal database.

3. Design flyers to announce your book: one for personal acquaintances, others geared toward bookstores, libraries, media, etc. Order paper, envelopes, and labels for mailing.

4. Mail news release, sales letter, and reviewer's request form to reviewers, covering those nationwide and those specific to your genre.

5. As reviewer requests come in, set them aside in a file until books arrive.

6. Review bluelines from printer carefully. Look for placement of type, page numbers, etc. This is not the time to proofread for spelling or grammatical errors.

7. Clear warehouse space and set up shipping area. Order shipping supplies and a postage scale.

8. Prepare sales materials: terms and conditions sheet for stores, sales flyer, discount schedule, etc.

9. Mail your prepublication offer to personal list with the joyous announcement of your book's publication date.

10. Stay in touch with your printer to find out when books will be shipped, when balance of money is due, etc. Be sure you will be there to accept shipment.

11. Request sample copies and ad rates from genre specific magazines and newsletters. Examine them and decide which you will send paid advertising to.

12. Write articles about your book and yourself for newsletters and magazines. Put names of magazines which are to receive review copies of the

172 Publish Your Own Novel

book on your database .

FIFTH—*The Big Day: The Books Arrive—3-4 months before pub date*

1. Laugh, weep, call all the neighbors, open champagne!

2. Take an inventory count while truck is still there to be sure all cartons arrived. Open a few cartons to be sure books are correct, not bound upside down or damaged.

3. Photograph book and have prints made, or use an extra cover and have postcards made.

4. Fill advance orders, and send out review copies and complimentary advance reading copies. Send finished copies to those prime reviewers who were sent galleys with follow-up letter requesting a tear sheet of their review.

5. Contact wholesalers and distributors who have not already signed you up.

6. Official paperwork: File copyright registration on form TX; send a copy of the book to the Library of Congress CIP office; send a copy to Cumulative Book Index; send a copy to Baker & Taylor and others listed in Appendix.

7. Carry a copy of your book with you at all times and have a case of books in your vehicle.

8. Contact all bookstores in your area.

9. Begin making plans for your author tour.

10. Scan cover to use as artwork in camera ready ads and flyers. Design ads for genre magazines and send to them.

11. Have pre publication party.

SIXTH — *The Pub Date*

1. Send media notices to newspapers, radio, and other sources in every town where you've ever lived.

2. Make up press kits with interview questions for radio stations.

3. Notify your Keylist of all booksignings and media appearances.

4. Sign up for writer's conferences or genre conferences for the coming year. Offer to appear on panels or sign books. Contact bookstores and media in the towns where conferences are held and arrange appearances in addition to the conference.

5. Mail flyers to bookstores, libraries, genre fans, organization memberships. Include an advertising specialty item like a pen or letter opener to get more attention.

6. Follow up with wholesalers to be sure books are available to stores.

7. Follow up with stores who received ARCs to see if they will order.

8. Collect copies of reviews as they come in. Update flyers for future mailings to include good quotes.

SEVENTH—*Ongoing Efforts—After pub date*
1. Keep your Keylist posted on your activities.
2. Continue to schedule booksignings as often as possible.
3. Start a revision file, listing typos and errors that should be corrected on a second printing.
4. Get busy on your second book!

Appendices

Help With Starting a Business

From general help to tax help, here are some guides that will be useful in starting your business. Nolo Press publishes a full line of business titles in addition to those listed here. Call 1-800-992-6656 for their catalog. Here are some of their titles:

Legal Guide for Starting and Running a Small Business
Tax Savvy for Small Business
Business Plans to Game Plans
How To Finance a Growing Business
How to Write a Business Plan
Marketing Without Advertising
The Employers Legal Handbook

Also see:
Law and the Writer, edited by Kirk Polking and Leonard S. Meranus; Writer's Digest Books
A guide to the complete copyright law, plus chapters on libel, invasion of privacy, subsidiary rights, entertainment law, and much more.

Starting and Operating a Business in (State); available for all 50 states, these guides give practical information on starting your business, with details pertaining to the applicable laws in your area. Widely available in bookstores.

Publisher Help

Great networking opportunities with other small presses. Most organizations offer monthly newsletters, conferences, co-op mailings, exhibit opportunities at major trade shows such as ABA and ALA. Check with each organization for specifics.

Organizations:

SPAN (Small Publishers Association of North America)
PO Box 1306
Buena Vista, CO 81211-1306

PMA (Publishers Marketing Association)
2401 Pacific Coast Highway, Ste 102
Hermosa Beach, CA 90254

Consultants:

About Books Inc.
Tom & Marilyn Ross
PO Box 1500
Buena Vista, CO 81211-1500
719-395-2459

The Ross's are authors of *The Complete Guide to Self Publishing*. Their company, About Books Inc., offers complete publishing services to small publishers, from editing and critiquing to working with book printers and cover design.

Cypress House
155 Cypress St.
Fort Bragg, CA 95437
707-964-9520

Complete production services, editing, rewriting, typesetting, design & illustration, cover art, printing, marketing & promotion, distribution & fulfillment. Any or all.

International Small Press Publishing Institute
121 E. Front St, Ste 401
Traverse City, MI 49684
The Institute produces two professional publishing semi-nars per year, spring and fall, where top pros present work-shops in pre-press, printing, distribution, sub-rights, promotion and more.

International Titles
Loris Essary, Dir.
931 East 56th St.
Austin, TX 78751-1724
512-451-2221
Trade show exhibit service. They cover all the major book shows, here and overseas. Reasonable rates, and they provide listings of potential buyers after the show.

Important Pre-pub and After Pub Lists

Send Advance Book Information

Baker & Taylor Books
PO Box 6920
Bridgewater, NJ 08807-0920
908-218-0400
Julia Quinones

Ingram Book Co.
PO Box 3006
La Vergne, TN 37086-1986
615-793-5000
Wanda Smith

Brodart Co.
500 Arch St.
Williamsport, PA 17705
717-326-2461
Mary Markle

Dustbooks
PO Box 100
Paradise, CA 95967-9999

R.R. Bowker Data Collection Center
PO Box 2068
Oldsmar, FL 34677-0037

Send Finished Books

Library of Congress, CIP Division
101 Independence Ave. SE
Washington, DC 20540-4320
(1 book with copy of LCCN form)

Register of Copyrights
Copyright Office
Library of Congress
Washington, DC 20559-6000
(2 books with copyright form TX)

American Book Publishing Record
R.R. Bowker Company
121 Chanlon Road
New Province, NJ 07974

Cumulative Book Index
H.W. Wilson Company
950 University Ave.
Bronx, NY 10452

Author Promotion Items

For inexpensive photo reprints
Duplicate Photo Labs
PO Box 2670
Hollywood, CA 90028
213-466-7544

Quality Photo Lab
5432 Hollywood Blvd.
Los Angeles, CA 90027
213-467-6178

Producers Photo Lab
6660 Santa Monica Blvd.
Los Angeles, CA 90038
213-462-1334

For advertising specialties
The Write Type, Inc.
P.O. Box 416
Angel Fire, NM 87710
505-377-6777
Offers a wide range of items including ballpoint pens, letter openers, caps, visors, drink cups and many other items that can be tailored to the theme of your book.

Media

Radio-TV Interview Report
Bradley Communications Corp.
135 E. Plumstead Ave. #129
Lansdowne, PA 19050
A place to advertise your availability as an interviewee.

Gale Research Inc.
835 Penobscot Bldg.
Detroit, MI 48226-4094
800-877-GALE (customer service)
800-347-GALE (editorial)
Publishes many excellent reference books of interest to publishers, including *The Directory of Special Libraries, Gale Directory of Publications,* and *Directory of Publications and Broadcast Media.* You can order mailing lists from Gale of any specific lists you want, or find these publications in most libraries. To find out all the directories that might be of interest, consult Gales' *Directory of Directories.*

Columnists and Commentators

See the Subject Index to Columnists and Commentators in *Literary Market Place* to find those columnists interested in your particular subject. Again, most of these will not interview fiction authors unless: a) you are a bestseller; or b) you have a newsworthy angle that ties your book to current events. Look for that angle, then find those columnists who cover it.

   * Denotes Primary Reviewers. Send galleys 4-5 months before pub date.

Forrest J. Ackerman
2495 Glendower Ave.
Hollywood, CA 90027-1110
Does national and international magazine and newspaper columns on books and films, particularly sci-fi, horror, and fantasy tie-ins.

American Book Publishing Record
R.R. Bowker
121 Chanlon Rd.
New Providence, NJ 07974
Contact: Beverley Lamar
Reviews 3,000 books/month

The American News Syndicate
58 Parry Rd.
Stamford, CT 06907
Book Ed: Richard K. Meyer
Reviews 1000 books/yr running the gamut of publishing

AudioFile
PO Box 109
Portland, ME 04112-0109
Reviews audio books, 40 per issue

John Austin
Hollywood Inside Syndicate
Box 49957
Los Angeles, CA 90049-0957
Syndicated to 84 weekly newspapers in the US and worldwide. Does "Books of the Week" book reviews and some author interviews on National Public Radio.

Joseph Barbato
5361 Tancy Ave.
Alexandria, VA 22304
Reviews books on all subjects. Columnist for "Independent Publishing" and contributing editor for *Publisher's Weekly*. Reviews and author interviews for *The Chronicle of Higher Education, Smithsonian, The Progressive* and *Inflight* magazines.

John Blades
Chicago Tribune
435 N. Michigan Ave.
Chicago, IL 60611
Does book features. Articles syndicated by Knight/Ridder.

The Bloomsbury Review
Owaissa Communications Co. Inc.
Tom Auer, Publisher
1028 Bannock
Denver, CO 80204
Book reviews, author interviews, reviews 100 books/issue

Book Links
Barbara Elleman, Ed. in Chief
50 E. Huron St.
Chicago, IL 60611-2795
Articles thematically designed around children's books. Annual
listing of good children's books.

Book Review Digest
Martha Mooney, Editor
H.W. Wilson Co.
950 University Ave.
Bronx, NY 10452
Reviews 7,000 books a year. Subscription service sold to 99 peri-
odicals and journals.

Book Week
Henry Kisor, Books Ed.
Chicago Sun-Times
401 N. Wabash Ave.
Chicago, IL 60611
Reviews 6 books per issue plus 2 genre roundups.

Book World
The Washington Post
1150 15 St. NW
Washington, DC 20071
Reviews 2,000 books per year in weekly literary section

*Booklist
American Library Association
50 E. Huron St.
Chicago, IL 60611
John Mort, Adult Books Editor
Ilene Cooper, Children's Books Editor
This is a major review source if you hope to sell to libraries

The Bookwatch
Midwest Book Review
Diane C. Donovan, Editor
166 Miramar Ave.
San Francisco, CA 94112
Reviews large and small press books, fiction and nonfiction, audios
and videos. Also online at Bookwatch.com. Reviews 800 books a
year.

Millicent Braverman
1517 Schuyler Rd.
Beverly Hills, CA 90210
Radio and TV interviews, "A Word on Books."

The Bulletin of the Center for Children's Books
University of Chicago
Betsy Hearne, Editor
1512 N. Fremont
Chicago, IL 60622
Reviews 900 juvenile books/year

Ann Casa
Book Chatter
PO Box 184
Bath Beach Sta.
Brooklyn, NY 11214

Children's Book Review Service
Ann Kalkhoff, Editor
220 Berkeley Place, Ste 1-D
Brooklyn, NY 11217
Reviews 775 children's and YA books per year.

Coast Book Review Service
Box 4174
Fullerton, CA 92634
Contacts: Don Cannon or Al Ralston
Reviews fiction and nonfiction semi-monthly in 125 daily and
weekly newspapers. Circulation 6 million.

Paul Craig
Box 15779
Sacramento, CA 95852
Thrice weekly presents "The Bookshelf" on books and authors.

Velma S. Daniels
1624 Lake Mirror Dr. NW
Winter Haven, FL 33881
"The Bookworm" weekly book column, radio show, daily TV program.

Digby Diehl
788 S. Lake Ave.
Pasadena, CA 91106
Daily columnist covering adult fiction and nonfiction, as well as children's books for the Prodigy computer network. Book columnist for *Good Morning America* and regular book columnist for *Modern Maturity* magazine.

Helen Dorsey
Family Circle Magazine and Editors Press Service
Woman's World
9239 Doheny Rd.
Los Angeles, CA 90069
In-depth interviews and entertainment articles.

Dusty Dog Reviews
1904-A Gladden
Gallup, NM 87301
Reviews poetry and chapbooks from small and mid-range presses.

Feminist Bookstore News
Carol Seajay, Editor
Box 882554
San Francisco, CA 94188
Reviews 1500 books per year. Useful if your book has a feminist slant.

Forecast
Baker & Taylor Books
652 E. Main St.
Box 6920
Bridgewater, NJ 08807-0920
Send prepublication announcements of all books. Circulation 11,000.

Rita Berman Frischer
9515 Gerald Ave.
Northridge North Hills, CA 91343
Book reviewer for *L.A. Jewish Journal*; children's book reviews for various publications; lecturer on children's literature; reviewer of other fiction and non-fiction.

Ralph Gardner's Bookshelf
Maturity News Service
135 Central Park W, Ste 5N
New York, NY 10023
Author interview articles on fiction and non-fiction. Hardcover and paperback. Books of interest to seniors syndicated to 200 newspapers nationwide.

Frances Halpern
Box 5657
Montecito, CA 93150
Does radio call-in show featuring the book industry. Interviews with editors, agents, writers.

*Kirkus Reviews
Anne Larsen, Book Review Editor
200 Park Ave. S.
New York, NY 10003
Prepublication reviews, 4,500 per year.

*Library Journal
Cahners Publishing Co.
Barbara Hoffert, Book Review Editor
249 W. 17th St.
New York, NY 10011
Important review source if you want to sell to libraries.

*New York Times Book Review
Rebecca Sinkler, Book Review Ed.
229 W. 43 St.
New York, NY 10036
Does prepublication reviews. Important to get galleys in early.

Joan Orth Syndicates
401 E. 65 St., Ste 14J
New York, NY 10021
Adult and Junior book reviews and author interviews. Syndicated to 20 radio stations in major book markets and 172 newspapers with combined circulation of 25.7 million.

Win Pendleton
Box 665
Windermere, FL 34786
Weekly book column and daily religious radio book review, "The Christian Book Shelf."

Poem Finder
Roth Publishing Inc.
185 Great Neck Rd.
Great Neck, NY 11021
A poetry index on CD-ROM. Reviews 1,000 books in each biennial issue.

*Publishers Weekly
Cahners Magazines
249 W. 17th St.
New York, NY 10011
(Look in the Forecasts section of the magazine to find out which editor to properly direct your galleys to.)
PW only publishes advance reviews. You must send galleys 4-5 months before pub date to have any hope of getting a review here.

Rave Reviews
c/o Romantic Times Publishing Group
163 Joralemon St.
Brooklyn Heights, NY 11201
In addition to romances, they review historicals, mysteries, thrillers, fantasy and sci-fi.

San Francisco Review of Books
Jennifer Martinez, Editor
555 De Haro St, Ste 220
San Francisco, CA 94107
Literary magazine, does book reviews, author interviews.

Curt Schleier
646 Jones Rd.
River Vale, NJ 07675
Twice-monthly columns with fiction and nonfiction forecasts, book industry news and author interviews.

*School Library Journal
Trevelyn Jones, Book Review Ed.
Cahners Magazines
249 W. 17th St.
New York, NY 10011
The children's and YA version of *Library Journal*. Reviews 3,750 books per year to the library market.

Derek Shearer
655 Ashland
Santa Monica, CA 90405
Reviews, among other topics, mysteries and thrillers for *L.A. Times, The Nation, Mother Jones* and others.

The Small Press Book Review
Henry Berry, Editor
Box 176
Southport, CT 06490
Reviews all types of books by small presses.

Small Press Review
Len Fulton, Book Review Editor
Box 100
Paradise, CA 95967

Bill Southwell - Books
National News Bureau
PO Box 43039
Philadelphia, PA 19129
Book reviews syndicated to 300 publications.

Barry Steinman
PO Box 4201
Carlsbad, CA 92018
Monthly columnist in Christian newspaper on inspirational topics.

San Francisco Chronicle Book Review Supplement
Patricia Holt, Book Review Ed.
901 Mission St.
San Francisco, CA 94103
Reviews and interviews of all types. Reviews 1,000 books per year.

Women's Review of Books
Linda Gardiner, Editor
Wellesley College Center for Research on Women
Wellesley, MA 02181
Reviews 20-30 books per month, by and about women.

Movie/TV Sources

Agents
Look in Literary Market Place for other names

The Gersch Agency
130 West 42nd St. #2400
New York, NY 10036-7802
212-997-1818   or:
The Gersch Agency
232 N. Canon Drive
Beverly Hills, CA 90210-5385
310-274-6611

International Creative Management
40 West 57th St.
New York, NY 10019-4070
212-556-5600

William Morris Agency
1350 Avenue of the Americas
New York, NY 10019-4864
212-586-5100 or:
William Morris Agency
151 El Camino Dr.
Beverly Hills, CA 90212
310-556-2727

Guides to the Entertainment Industry
The Acquisitions and Development Directory
ADD Publishing
12021 Wilshire Blvd #459
Los Angeles, CA 90025
213-460-2544

Film Producers, Studios, and Agents Guide
Lone Eagle Publishing
2337 Roscomare Rd.
Los Angeles, CA 90077
310-471-8066

Who's Who in Entertainment
Who's Who in Television
available at most libraries

Television Networks

ABC-TV
2040 Avenue of the Stars, 7th Fl.
Century City, CA 90067
310-557-7777

ABC-TV
77 West 66th St.
New York, NY 10023

American Movie Classics
150 Crossways Park W.
Woodbury, NY 11797
516-364-2222

Arts & Entertainment Network
235 E. 45th St.
New York, NY 10017

Black Entertainment Television
1899 Ninth St.
Washington, DC 20018

Cable News Network
WTBS
1050 Techwood Dr. NW
Atlanta, GA 30318
404-827-1895

Cinemax, HBO
1100 Avenue of the Americas
New York, NY 10036
212-512-1208

CBS-TV
7800 Beverly Blvd.
Los Angeles, CA 90036
213-852-2345

CBS-TV
51 West 52nd St.
New York, NY 10023

CNBC
2200 Fletcher Ave.
Ft. Lee, NJ 07024
201-346-2136

Discovery Channel, Learning Channel
7700 Wisconsin Ave.
Bethesda, MD 20814-3522
301-986-1999

Disney Channel
4111 W. Alameda Ave.
Burbank, CA 91505

ESPN
ESPN Plaza
935 Middle St.
Bristol, CT 06010
203-585-2000

Family Channel
2877 Guardian Lane
PO Box 2050
Virginia Beach, VA 23452
804-459-6000

Fox Broadcasting
10201 West Pico Blvd.
Los Angeles, CA 90035
310-203-3553

Lifetime
36-12 35th Ave.
Astoria, NY 11106

MTV, Nickelodeon
1515 Broadway
New York, NY 10036
212-258-8000

Nashville Network
2806 Opryland Dr.
Nashville, TN 37214
615-889-6840

NBC-TV
3000 W. Alameda
Burbank, CA 91523
818-840-4444

NBC-TV
30 Rockefeller Plaza
New York, NY 10112
212-664-4444

Nostalgia Channel
71 West 23rd St., Ste 502
New York, NY 10010

Showtime, The Movie Channel
1633 Broadway
New York, NY ??
212-708-1600

USA Network
1230 Avenue of the Americas
New York, NY 10020
212-408-9166

Vision Interfaith Satellite Network
74 Trinity Place, Ste 800
New York, NY 10016
800-552-5131

Book Clubs - General

See genre listings for those specific to your genre

Book of the Month Club Inc.
Subs of Time Warner Inc.
Time & Life Bldg.
1271 Avenue of the Americas
New York, NY 10020-2686
212-522-4200
BOMC actually has eight book clubs, with 3.1 million members.
Contact them to find out which editor is right for your type of books.

Books of Light
14230 Phillips Rd.
Alpharetta, GA 30201
Leslie Swanson
404-664-4886
Among other subjects, Books of Light carries fantasy and sci-fi and
fine literature titles.

Classics Club
Div. of Walter J. Black Inc.
20 W. Vanderventer Ave.
Port Washington, NY 11050
Ed-in-chief: Theodore M Black Sr.
Carries literary classics

Doubleday Book Club
401 Franklin Ave.
Garden City, NY 11530-5945
Ed-in-Chief: Sam Blum
516-873-4561

Literary Guild
401 Franklin Ave.
Garden City, NY 11530-5945
Ed-in-Chief: Karen Daly
516-873-4561

Military Book Club
Subs of Doubleday Book & Music Clubs Inc.
401 Franklin Ave.
Garden City, NY 11530-5945
Ed: Moshe Feder
516-873-4801
(Note: We placed this listing under general, since military novels
might fit into several categories.)

Quality Paperback Book Club
Book-of-the-Month-Club Inc.
Time & Life Bldg.
1271 Avenue of the Americas
New York, NY 10020
Sr. Ed.: David Rosen

Reader's Digest Condensed Books
Div of Reader's Digest Association Inc.
Reader's Digest Rd.
Pleasantville, NY 10570
Ed.-in-chief: Barbara J. Morgan
914-238-1000

Book Wholesalers and Distributors

Find more listings in *Literary Market Place*.

Atrium Publishers Group
3356 Coffey Lane
Santa Rosa, CA 95403

Baker & Taylor Books
Publisher Services
PO Box 6920
Bridgewater, NJ 08807

Blackwell North America, Inc.
100 University Court
Blackwood, NJ 08012

The Book House, Inc.
208 W. Chicago St.
Jonesville, MI 49250-0125

Brodart Company
500 Arch St.
Williamsport, PA 17705

Coutts Library Service Inc.
1823 Maryland Ave.
PO Box 1000
Niagara Falls, NY 14302-1000

Eastern Book Co.
131 Middle Street
Portland, ME 04101

Emery-Pratt Company
1966 W. Main St.
Owosso, MI 48867-1372

Independent Publishers Group
814 N. Franklin St.
Chicago, IL 60610

Ingram Book Company
PO Box 3006
La Vergne, TN 37086

Inland Book Company
PO Box 120261
East Haven, CT 06512

Midwest Library Service
11443 St. Charles Rock Rd.
Bridgeton, MO 63044-2789

Pacific Pipeline
8030 S. 228
Kent, WA 98032

Publishers Group West
4065 Hollis St.
Emeryville, CA 94608

Yankee Book Peddler
999 Maple St.
Contoocook, NH 03229-3374

Chain Bookstores

Barnes & Noble
Marcella Smith
122 Fifth Ave.
New York, NY 10011

Walden Books
Stuart Carter, East Coast Regional Buyer
515 E. Liberty St.
Ann Arbor, MI 48104

Walden Books
Helen Ibach, West Coat Regional Buyer
515 E. Liberty St.
Ann Arbor, MI 48104

Borders
Diana Calice
515 E. Liberty St.
Ann Arbor, MI 48104

Musicland
Doug Cline
10400 Yellow Circle Dr.
Minnetoonka, MN 55343-9134

Lauriats
Julie Barton
10 Pequot Way
Canton, MA 02021

Chain Book Stores, cont'd
Tower Books
Heidi Cotler
PO Box 1700
West Sacramento, CA 95691

Rizzoli
Michael Gray
300 Park Ave. South
New York, NY 10010

Large Library Systems

This is just a sampling of some of the larger library systems in the country. You can rent specialized library mailing lists from R.R. Bowker or other mailing list companies. Also, your genre association may have lists of libraries that have large collections of your particular type of book. Be sure to address your mailing to the Fiction Acquisitions Librarian.

New York Public Library
8 E. 40th St.
New York, NY 10016

Brooklyn Public Library
Grand Army Plaza
Brooklyn, NY 11238

Nassau Library System
900 Jerusalem Ave.
Uniondale, NY 11553

Monmouth County Library
125 Symmes Drive
Manalapan, NJ 07726

Somerset County Library
PO Box 6700
Bridgewater, NJ 08807

San Diego Public Library
820 "E" Street
San Diego, CA 92101

Los Angeles Public Library
361 S. Anderson St.
Los Angeles, CA 90033

Long Beach Public Library
101 Pacific Ave.
Long Beach, CA 90802

Santa Clara County Library
1091 North 7th St.
San Jose, CA 95112

Fort Worth Public Library
300 Taylor St.
Fort Worth, TX 76102-7333

Houston Public Library
500 McKinney Ave.
Houston, TX 77002

Dallas Public Library
1515 Young
Dallas, TX 75201

Phoenix Public Library
Bibliographic Services
1221 N. Central Ave.
Phoenix, AZ 85004

Boston Public Library
PO Box 286
Boston, MA 02117

Atlanta-Fulton Public Library
1 Margaret Mitchell Sq. NW
Atlanta, GA 30303

Lexington Public Library
140 E. Main St.
Lexington, KY 40507

Chicago Public Library
1224 W. Van Buren
Chicago, IL 60607

Detroit Public Library
5201 Woodward Ave.
Detroit, MI 48202

McKinley Memorial Library
40 North Main St.
Niles, OH 44446

Free Library of Philadelphia
Logan Square
1901 Vine St.
Philadelphia, PA 19103

Internet Sites

Amazon.com
http:www.amazon.com
The world's largest bookstore with 1.1 million titles. Creates free custom web pages. Color cover art can be included for $26. To get more information e-mail content-dept@amazon.com

Book Stacks
http://www.books.com
The online bookstore. List all your titles plus book covers, author readings, reviews, and more. Call Angela Finet at 215-379-0907 or e-mail afinet@books.com

Book Wire
http://www.bookwire.com
Rated by *The Net Magazine* as an outstanding accomplishment that should pique the interest of book lovers and the publishing industry. Call 800-226-6594 or e-mail advertising@bookwire.com

Book Zone
http://www.bookzone.com
Award-winning provider of Internet services to more than 450 publishers. Will put your entire catalog online. Call 800-536-6162

Kingswood Interactive
http://www.kingswood.com/kad/
Home pages, online promotions, 'net catalogs, web-based publicity. Call Rick Moore 800-950-3906

There are also numerous online chat groups in every special interest category. See Chapters 6 and 8 for ideas.

Office Supplies

Viking Office Products
PO Box 61144
Los Angeles, CA 90061-0144
800-421-1222

Quill Corporation
PO Box 94080
Palatine, IL 60094-4080
800-789-8965

Mailing Supplies

Arrow Star Discount
6087 Buford Hwy, Dept S
Norcross, GA 30071
800-645-2982

BrownCor International
PO Box 04499
Milwaukee, WI 53204
800-327-2278

Chiswick Trading, Inc.
1414 Twelfth St. NW
Albuquerque, NM 87104
800-225-8708

U-Line
950 Albrecht Drive
Lake Bluff, IL 60044
800-295-5510

Stationery, Business Cards, etc.

Viking Office Products
PO Box 61144
Los Angeles, CA 90061-0144
800-421-1222

NEBS, Inc.
500 Main St.
Groton, MA 01471
800-225-6380

RapidForms
301 Grove Rd.
Thorofare, NJ 08086-9499
800-257-8354

Wholesale Printing Service
PO Box 1414
Bristol, TN 37621
(Inexpensive business cards, stationery, rubber stamps, and post-cards. Basic layouts only, but good prices.)

Specialty Papers for brochures, flyers, etc.

Idea Art Impact
PO Box 291505
Nashville, TN 37229-1505
800-433-2278

Paper Direct
100 Plaza Drive
Secaucus, NJ 07094-3606
800-A-PAPERS

Quill
100 Schelter Rd.
Lincolnshire, IL 60069-3621
800-789-5813

ICON Graphix
6460 N. Lincoln Ave.
Lincolnwood, IL 60645
800-ICON-121

Premier Papers Inc.
PO Box 64785
St. Paul, MN 55164

Computers and Computer Supplies

Global Computer Supplies
2318 East Del Amo Blvd. Dept 71
Compton, CA 90220
800-845-6225

Micro Systems Warehouse
PO Box 3014
Lakewood, NJ 08701-3014
800-660-3222

Insight Direct Inc.
1912 West 4th St.
Tempe, AZ 85281
800-796-1111

Direct Ware
19951 Mariner Ave., Ste 100
Torrance, CA 90503
800-590-9273

CDW Computer Centers Inc.
1020 E. Lake Cook Rd.
Buffalo Grove, IL 60089
800-218-4CDW

Mailer's Software
970 Calle Negocio
San Clemente, CA 92673-6201
800-800-MAIL

Order Entry Software

Pacioli 2000
M-USA
18111 Preston Rd., Ste 500
Dallas, TX 75252

Publishers Business System
rh Communications
PO Box 26225
Colorado Springs, CO 80936-6225

Acumen Inc.
803 Juniper Lane
Santa Fe, NM 87501

The Cat's Pajamas
PO Box 1016
Anacortes, WA 98221

Peachtree
Quicken
QuickBooks
All commonly available at office supply and retail computer stores.

Book Manufacturers

Berryville Graphics
PO Box 272
Berryville, VA 22611
800-382-7249
(specializes in children's books)

BookCrafters
613 E. Industrial Dr.
Chelsea, MI 48118
313-475-9145 ext 244

BookMasters Inc.
Box 159
Ashland, OH 44805
419-289-6051
(will do as few as 100 books)

Braun-Brumfield Inc.
100 North Staebler Rd.
Ann Arbor, MI 48106
313-662-3291

C & M Press
4825 Nome St.
Denver, CO 80239
303-375-9922
(will do as few as 50 books)

Edwards Brothers Inc.
2500 S. State St.
Ann Arbor, MI 48106
313-769-1000 ext 317
(short to medium runs)

Gilliland Printing, Inc.
215 North Summit St.
Arkansas City, KS 67005
316-442-0500
(1,000 to 15,000 copies)

Marrakech Express
500 Anclote Rd.
Tarpon Springs, FL 34689
813-942-2218

McNaughton & Gunn, Inc.
PO Box 10
Saline, MI 48176
313-429-5411

Rose Printing Company Inc.
PO Box 5078
Tallahasse, FL 32314
904-576-4151

Thomson-Shore Inc.
7300 W. Joy Rd.
Dexter, MI 48130
313-426-3939
(will print as few as 100 books)

Audio Producers & Packagers

Tapette Corp.
5 Whatney
Irvine, CA 92718
714-588-7000

V-Corp
1228 East Edna Place
Covina, CA 90724
800-V-CORP-99

Rainbo Records & Cassettes
1738 Berkeley St.
Santa Monica, CA 90404
310-829-3476

Bookland EAN Scanning Symbol Suppliers

Fotel GGX
6 Grace Ave.
Great Neck, NY 11021
800-834-8088

International Artwork Service
1111 W. El Camino Real #109-316
Sunnyvale, CA 94087
800-528-3535

Laser Systems Service
11912 Rivera Rd. #H
Santa Fe Springs, CA 92691
310-907-6721

Graphic Artists

BJ Graphics
Barb Gunia
8811 Martz Rd.
Ypsilanti, MI 48197
313-482-8884

Gabriel Illustrations
Andrea Gabriel
1411 I Street #3
Bellingham, WA 98225
360-647-1044

Abacus Graphics
4701 Morning Canyon Rd.
Oceanside, CA 92056
619-724-7750

John Cole, Graphic Designer
3 Juego Place
Santa Fe, NM 87505
505-466-7311

C.C.S. Graphics Associate
Christina C. Santos
11755 Slauson Ave, Ste 1
Santa Fe Springs, CA 90670
310-695-1555

Joel Friedlander Publishing Services
Joel Friedlander
PO Box 3330
San Rafael, CA 94912
415-459-1311

Editorial Services

Also check with your own writer's groups. There are often members with editorial experience.

Book Doctor
Robyn Weaver
116 Brushy Nob
Joshua, TX 76058
817-558-6428

Critique for Hire
Judy Lewis
PO Box 4
Arvada, CO 80001-0004
303-431-8792

Peoplespeak
Sharon Goldinger
25342 Costeau
Laguna Hills, CA 92653
714-581-6190

Word for Word
Robin Quinn
310-838-7098
e-mail: quinnrobin@aol.com

Display Products

Clear Solutions
Box 2460
W. Brattleboro, VT 05303
603-256-6644

Hannecke Displays
300G Rt 17 S.
Mahwah, NJ 07430
800-345-8631

ABELexpress
230 East Main St.
Carnegie, PA 15106
800-542-9001

City Diecutting, Inc.
2 Babcock Place
West Orange, NJ 07052
201-736-1224

Traverse Bay Display Company
4366 Deerwood Dr.
Traverse City, MI 49686
800-240-9802

Color Printing of Postcards, Brochures, Posters, etc.

American Color Printing
1731 NW 97th Ave.
Plantation, FL 33322
305-473-4392

U.S. Press
PO Box 640
Valdosta, GA 31603-0640
800-227-7377

Remainder Dealers

These firms buy bulk remainder stock from publishers, usually at cost or below. The ones listed here specialize in a variety of books, including fiction.

Fairmount Books Ltd.
120 Duffield Dr.
Markham, ON L6G 1B5
Canada
416-475-0988

Faro House
404 Court St.
Binghamton, NY 13904
607-723-0370

Little Dania's Juvenile Promotions
Booksmith Promotional Co.
100 Paterson Plank Rd.
Jersey City, NJ 07307
201-659-2317
(Juvenile titles)

Remainder Dealers, cont'd
Marboro Books Inc.
One Pond Rd.
Rockleigh, NJ 07647
201-784-4264

S.A.V.E. Half Price Books for Libraries
PO Box 30
Schulenburg, TX 78956-0030
409-743-4147

True Remainders Ltd.
Box 500 Jordan Station
ON L0R 1S0
Canada
416-562-7767

Fulfillment Services

The following companies cater specifically to small publishers. Many offer 800# ordering for your customers as well as invoicing and collection of receivables. Contact them for a complete description of services. For additional listings, see *Literary Market Place*.

Arcata Graphics Distribution
Subs of Arcata Graphics Co.
Box 1968
Kingsport, TN 37662
615-357-2000

BookCrafters Distribution Center
Div. of Bookcrafters Inc.
615 E. Industrial Dr.
Chelsea, MI 48118
313-475-1374

Custom Packaging Co.
Bldg 3, Brooklyn Navy Yard
Brooklyn, NY 11205
718-834-0172

Mercedes Distribution Center Inc.
62 Imlay St.
Brooklyn, NY 11231
718-522-7111

Mid-Atlantic Book Service Inc.
5 Lawrence St.
Bloomfield, NJ 07003
201-429-7530

Midpoint National Inc.
2215 Harrison St.
Kansas City, MO 64108
816-842-8420

Package Fulfillment Center Inc.
1401 Lakeland Ave.
Behemia, NY 11716
516-567-7000

Publishers Storage & Shipping Corp.
46 Development Rd.
Fitchburg, MA 01420
508-345-2121

STCS Book Distribution Services
PO Box 246
Glassboro, NJ 08028
609-863-1030

Publications of Interest

Trade Magazines:

Advertising Age
Crain Communications
220 E. 42nd St.
New York, NY 10017
Weekly magazine covering advertising in magazines, trade journals and business.

Poets & Writers
72 Spring St.
New York, NY 10012
Monthly magazine, primarily for literary writers and poets.

Publisher's Weekly
249 W. 17th St.
New York, NY 10011
Weekly magazine covering the book publishing industry. Recommended for all publishers.

The Writer
120 Boylston St.
Boston, MA 02116
Monthly writer's magazine.

Writer's Digest
1507 Dana Ave.
Cincinnati, OH 45207
Monthly writer's magazine.

Small Publisher
Nigel Maxey, Editor
Box 1620
Pineville, WV 24874

Books and Directories:

The Complete Guide to Self Publishing by Marilyn and Tom Ross, Writer's Digest Books, 1507 Dana Ave, Cincinnati, OH 45207

Copyright Handbook, R.R. Bowker, A Reed Reference Publishing Co, 121 Chanlon Rd., New Providence, NJ 07974

Directory of Editorial Resources, Editorial Experts Inc., 66 Canal Center Plaza, Ste 200, Alexandria, VA 22314-1538

The Guide to Writers Conferences, ShawGuides, 625 Biltmore Way, Ste 1406, Coral Gables, FL 33134

International Directory of Little Magazines and Small Presses, edited by Len Fulton, Dustbooks, PO Box 100, Paradise, CA 95967 (recommended place to have your press listed)

Literary Market Place and *International Literary Market Place*, R.R. Bowker, A Reed Reference Publishing Co, 121 Chanlon Rd., New Providence, NJ 07974

Writer's Market, updated each year, Writer's Digest Books, 1057 Dana Ave, Cincinnati, OH 45207 (good place to locate sources for subsidiary rights)

Help With Promotion and Marketing

The Writer's Guide to Self-Promotion and Publicity, by Elane Feldman, Writer's Digest Books, 1507 Dana Ave, Cincinnati, OH 45207

1001 Ways to Market Your Books by John Kremer, Open Horizons, PO Box 205, Fairfield, IA 52556-0205 (also available through Writer's Digest Books)

The Unabashed Self-Promoter's Guide by Dr. Jeffrey Lant, JLA Publications, 50 Follen St, Ste 507, Cambridge, MA 02138

Co-op Mailings and Mailing List Brokers

Also look in your phone book's yellow pages under Mailing Lists

Publishers Marketing Association
2401 Pacific Coast Hwy, Ste 102
Hermosa Beach, CA 90254
310-372-2732
Does co-op mailings and catalog mailings to libraries, bookstores, reviewers and targeted markets. Also staffs exhibits at the major trade shows at very reasonable costs. Must be a member to use these services.

Association of Canadian Publishers
2 Gloucester St. Ste 301
Toronto, ON M4Y 1L5 Canada
416-413-4929
Mailing lists of Canadian newspapers, TV, radio, magazines, wire services, news directors, book review editors, advertising directors and more.

Twin Peaks Press
PO Box 129
Vancouver, WA 98666
360-694-2462
Co-op mailings to targeted lists of libraries, bookstores, and other
book industry lists.

Lawco Ltd.
PO Box 2009
Manteca, CA 95336-1209
Co-op mailing lists to libraries.

R.R. Bowker Lists
John Panza
245 W. 17th St.
New York, NY 10011
212-337-7164

J-Mart Press
409 King Richard Dr.
Virginia Beach, VA 23450
804-487-4060
Co-op mailings

In One Ear
29481 Manzanita Dr.
Campo, CA 91906-1128
619-478-5619
Co-op mailings

Publicists

Also see *Literary Market Place* under the heading Public Relations Services. Those listed here are a few who specifically handle fiction authors.

Alice B. Acheson
3362 Laguna St.
San Francisco, CA 94123-2208
415-563-5122

Allen Communications Group Inc.
770 Lexington Ave.
New York, NY 10021
212-755-4545

Barnes Communications Inc.
19 W. 44th St., Ste 705
New York, NY 10036
212-302-3399

Lisl Cade Communications
172 W. 79th St.
New York, NY 10024
212-595-6225

Kaufman Communications
12 E. 86th St., Ste 831
New York, NY 10028
212-988-0506

Susan Magrino Agency
167 E. 73rd St.
New York, NY 10021
212-744-2004

One Potata Productions Inc.
197 Bleecker St,
New York, NY 10012
212-353-3478

Planned Television Arts Ltd.
Subs of PTA Ltd.
25 W. 43rd St.
New York, NY 10036
212-921-5111

Raab Associates
19 Price's Lane
Rose Valley, PA 19065
215-565-8188
specializes in children's book promotions

Ira Silverberg
401 W. Broadway, Ste 1
New York, NY 10012
specializes in literary fiction

Jane Wesman Public Relations
928 Broadway, Ste 903
New York, NY 10010
212-598-4440

Writer's Conferences - Not Genre Specific

Note: These conferences were scheduled in 1996 and may or may not be annual events. For a large listing of conferences nationwide, see the Annual Writer's Conference issue of *Writer's Digest* magazine.

Stonecoast Writers Conference, University of Southern Maine, Office of Extended Academic Programs, 96 Famouth St., Portland, ME 04103, 207-780-4076, Late July. Credit or non-credit workshops in short fiction, non-fiction, novel, genre writing, and poetry.

"The Flight of the Mind" Writing workshops for Women. Mid-June. Poetry, fiction, memoir, screenwriting. Send SASE to 622 SE 29th, Portland, OR 97214

Santa Barbara Writers Conference. Mid-June. An exciting week of workshops with pros from all genre. Write Mary or Barnaby Conrad, Box 304, Carpinteria, CA 93014

Aspen Writers Conference. Late June. Features lectures, readings, workshops, tutorials, and social events. Contact the Aspen Writers' Foundation, Drawer 7726, Aspen, CO 81612

Arkansas Writers' Conference. Early June. Nearly 50 writing awards are presented. Contact Clovita Rice, AWC Director, 1115 Gillette Dr., Little Rock, AR 72207

Ocooch Mountain Writers' Retreat. Early July. Poetry and fiction workshops in a peaceful rural setting in Southwestern Wisconsin. Write UWC-Richland, 1200 Hwy 14 West, Richland Center, WI 53581.

Santa Fe Writers' Conference. Early August. Workshops in fiction, poetry and screenwriting. Talks by literary agents and editors, individual conferences. Contact: Director, Santa Fe Writers' Conference, Recursos de Santa Fe, 826 Camino de Monte Rey, Santa Fe, NM 87501.

Sewanee Writers' Conference. Mid to late July. Workshops in poetry, fiction and playwriting featuring well-known writers. Contact Conference Administrator, Sewanee Writers' Conference, 310R St. Luke's Hall, 735 University Ave. Sewanee, TN 37383-1000.

Iowa Summer Writing Festival. Mid June to end of July. Offering 90 non-credit workshops lasting a weekend, a week, or two weeks. Topics include poetry, essay, novel, novella, children's stories, columns, TV writing, romance, memoir and more. Emphasis on small classes with feedback from instructor and students. Contact Peggy Houston, Director, Division of Continuing Education, University of Iowa, 116 International Center, Iowa City, IA 52242-1802.

"First Vision" Bozeman Writers' Retreat. Early August. Workshops in fiction and poetry. Contact: First Vision, Institutes and Conferences, 204 Culbertson, MSU, Bozeman, MT 59717

Napa Valley Writers' Conference. Late July-early August. A week of small intensive workshops devoted to generating new poetry and exploring the craft of fiction. Contact: NV Writers' Conference, Napa Valley College, 2277 Napa-Vallejo Hwy, Napa, CA 94558.

Mount Holyoke Writers' Conference. Early June. Workshops, lectures, panels, and private conferences with well-known writers. Contact: Michael Pettit, Director, Mount Holyoke Writers' Conference, Box 3213-D, Mount Holyoke College, South Hadley, MA 01075.

Rope Walk Writers Retreat. Mid June. Workshops, conferences, and writing time in the historic setting of two 19th century utopias. Contact: English Department, Univ. of Southern Indiana, Evansville, IN 47712.

Bread Loaf Writers' Annual Conference. Mid August. Featuring well-known writers and teachers. Contact: Mrs. Carol Knauss, The Bread Loaf Writers' Conference, Middlebury College, Middlebury, VT 05753-6125.

Imagination: A Writers' Conference and Workshop. Mid July. From poetry to novels, from science-fiction to mainstream realism. Workshops, classes, readings. Contact: English Department, Cleveland State University, Cleveland, OH 44115.

Taos School of Writing. Mid July. Classes in fiction and non-fiction taught by well-known writers and teachers. Fee includes tuition, meals and room. Contact: Taos School of Writing, PO Box 20496, Albuquerque, NM 87154.

Wesleyan Writers Conference. Late June. Novel, short story, poetry, fiction techniques, and more. Staff includes well-known writers and teachers. Contact: Anne Greene, Director, Wesleyan Writers Conference, Wesleyan University, Middletown, CT 06459.

Yellow Bay Writers Workshop. Mid August. Informal setting on Flathead Lake in western Montana. Fiction, non-fiction, poetry and craft. Contact: YBWW, Center of Continuing Education, University of Montana, Missoula, MT 59812.

Antioch Writers' Workshop of Yellow Springs. Late July. Work with a community of writers. Contact: Susan Carpenter, PO Box 494, Yellow Springs, OH 45387.

Indiana University Annual Writers' Conference. Mid June. Poetry, fiction and mixed workshops, classes, readings, panels. Contact: The IU Writers' Conference, 464 Ballantine Hall, Bloomington, IN 47405.

Cape Cod Writers' Center's Annual Conference. Late August. Workshops on fiction, non-fiction, writing for juveniles, writing for TV and film. Also personal conferences, MS evaluation, exhibits, bookstore, lectures by noted authors. Contact: Marion Vuilleumier, Executive Director, Cape Cod Writer's Center a/o Conservatory Rte 132 W, Barnstable, MA 02668.

American Society of Journalists and Authors Annual Conference. Early June. Choose from 25 workshops. Contact: ASJ&A, 1501 Broadway, Ste 302W, New York, NY 10036.

Port Townsend Annual Writers' Conference. Mid July. Contact: Centrum, PO Box 1158, Port Townsend, WA 98368.

M.E. Hughes's Peripatetic Writing Workshop and Colony. Month of July. In-depth editing of novels, weekly workshops and tutorials. Limited number of attendees. Send SASE to M.E. Hughes, PO Box 822, Village Station, New York, NY 10014.

Southwest Writers Workshop's Annual Conference. Late August. Keynote speakers, contest awards, many workshops and classes on all aspects of writing. Editors and agents, personal appointments. Contact: Southwest Writers Workshop, 1338-B Wyoming Blvd NE, Albuquerque, NM 87112.

Writer/Publisher Organizations, Awards, Conferences — By Genre

Children's—Genre References

Society of Children's Book Writers and Illustrators
22736 Vanowen St, Ste 106
West Hills, CA 91307

Membership classes: Full membership for published writers, Dues $50/year
Associate membership for anyone interested in children's literature, published or not, Dues $50/year

The SCBWI acts as a network for the exchange of knowledge between writers, illustrators, editors, publishers, agents, librarians, educators, bookstore personnel and others involved with literature for young people. Benefits include SCBWI's voice as a professional guild for writers and illustrators, its advisory function for all members, its bimonthly newsletter, the SCBWI *Bulletin*, meetings, awards, grants, and an annual conference.

Awards and Grants: The Golden Kite Awards in three categories, Magazine Merit Awards in three categories, Work-in-Progress Grants, Don Freeman Memorial Grant-in-Aid, Barbara Karlin Grant.

Annual Conference: Held each year in August. Brings luminaries in the field to provide lectures, workshops, and individual consultation for attendees. Several smaller regional conferences also take place.

Children's Book Council
568 Broadway, Ste 404
New York, NY 10012

The Children's Book Council is a non-profit trade association of children's book publishers. The purpose of the Council
is to promote the use and enjoyment of children's trade books
and to disseminate information about books for young people
and about trade book publishing.

Membership is open to all U.S. children's book publishers.
Personal memberships are not available, although individuals, organizations and institutions can be added to the mailing
list to receive newsletters, brochures, and information on
activities for a one-time fee of $60.

The CBC sponsors National Children's Book Week in
November each year. They offer an extensive list of free or
low-cost publications geared toward those in the children's
book business.

Other Resources:
Children's Book Review Magazine
Anita Sorenson, Editor
PO Box 5082
Brentwood, TN 37024-9767
Secular magazine that features reviews on children's books

China Berry Book Service
2780 Via Orange Way, Ste B
Spring Valley, CA 91978
Service that sells children's books by direct mail.

Horn Book Magazine
14 Beacon St.
Boston, MA 02108
Bimonthly magazine that covers children's literature.

Book Clubs:

Arrow Book Club
Scholastic Inc.
730 Broadway
New York, NY 10003
Ed: Pat Brigandi
212-505-3215
Grades 4-6

Augsburg Fortress Reading Club
Div. of Augsburg Fortress Publishers
Box 1209
Minneapolis, MN 55440
Religious books for adults, young adults & children

Books of My Very Own
Book-of-the-Month Club Inc.
Time Life Bldg
1271 Avenue of the Americas
New York, NY 10020
Sr. Ed. Children's Books: Steve Geck
212-522-4200
Hardcover and softcover books, from babies to age 10

Children's Book Club
1540 Broadway, 23rd Fl.
New York, NY 10036
Ed-in-Chief: Miranda de Kay
212-782-7269

Children's Book-of-the-Month Club
Book-of-the-Month Club Inc.
Time Life Bldg
1271 Avenue of the Americas
New York, NY 10020
Sr. Ed. Children's Books: Steve Geck
212-522-4200
Four age groups, from babies to age 12

Early Start
Newbridge Communications Inc.
333 E. 38 St.
New York, NY 10016
Manag. Dir: Marilyn Karp
212-455-5000
Storybooks and board books for children 6 months to 2 years.

Firefly Book Club
Scholastic Inc.
730 Broadway
New York, NY 10003
Ed: Lauren Stevens
212-505-3000
Preschool children ages 0-5

Junior Library Guild
1540 Broadway
New York, NY 10036
Dir: Marjorie Jones
212-782-8943
Hardcover books for seven age groups, preschool through high school

Lucky Book Club
Scholastic Inc.
730 Broadway
New York, NY 10003
Sr. Ed: Eva Moore
212-505-3000
Paperbound reprints and originals for grades 2-3

See-Saw Book Club
Scholastic Inc.
730 Broadway
New York, NY 10003
Ed: Erin McCormack
212-505-3217
Paperbound reprints and hardcover and paperbound originals for
grades K-1

Teen Age Book Club
Scholastic Inc.
730 Broadway
New York, NY 10003
Ed: Greg Holch
212-505-3000
Paperbound reprints and originals for grades 7-12

Troll Book Clubs Inc.
100 Corporate Dr.
Mahwah, NJ 07430
Dir: Barbara Rittenhouse
201-529-4000

Trumpet Club
Subs of Bantam Doubleday Dell
1540 Broadway
New York, NY 10036
Edit Dir: Susan Bishansky
212-354-6500
Top quality titles from all publishers on a wide variety of subjects.
Grades pre-K to 8

Weekly Reader Children's Book Clubs
Newfield Publications
245 Long Hill Rd.
Middletown, CT 06457
Edit Dir: Fritz Luecke
203-638-2400
Hardcover selections from all children's publishers. Three age
groups from ages 4 to 11.

Religious—Genre References

Christian Writers Guild
260 Fern Lane
Hume Lake, CA 93628-9999

The Christian Writers Guild's main purpose is providing a 48-lesson home study course. Writers who elect not to take the course may join the Guild for $45 a year. This includes their paper, *The Quill o' the Wisp* and offers members free consultation services on any manuscripts they wish to send.

Christian Writers Fellowship International
Rt 3, Box 1635 Jefferson Davis Road
Clinton, SC 29325

The Christian Writers Fellowship International is a multi-service organization for Christians in publishing. They inform, equip, and encourage writers.

Membership: $35 per year
Newsletter only: $18 per year

Membership includes the newsletter, *Cross and Quill*, access to critique and market consultation services, access to a database of writers, groups, and conferences, writers books, tapes, and resources, on-line services.

Numerous conferences take place in various regions, as described in their newsletter.

Other Resources:

Religion BookLine
Publisher's Weekly
PO Box 6457
Torrance, CA 90504-0457
Reviews of religious books, audios, videos and multimedia formats.

Interviews & Reviews
Three Central Plaza, Suite 355
Rome, GA 30161
New full color magazine that features interviews on well-known individuals and reviews on organizations, books, movies, and entertainment media.

Children's Book Review Magazine
Anita Sorenson, Editor
PO Box 5082
Brentwood, TN 37024-9767
Secular magazine that features reviews on children's books

The Guide to Religious and Inspirational Markets
Published by Writer's Resources
15 Margaret's Way
Nantucket, MA 02554
Lists magazines, newspapers, newsletters, and other serialized publications that use religious pieces. Indexes list publications by subject (i.e. fiction) as well as by religion and denomination to help you target those publications that might buy or review your type of work.

Book clubs:

Augsburg Fortress Reading Club
Div. of Augsburg Fortress Publishers
Box 1209
Minneapolis, MN 55440
Religious books for adults, young adults & children

Catholic Book Club
The America Press
106 W. 56th St.
New York, NY 10019
Chmn, Edit Bd: David S. Toolan
212-581-4640

Catholic Digest Book Club
Div. of University of St. Thomas
475 Riverside Dr. Ste 1268
New York, NY 10115
Ed: Henry Lexau

China Berry Book Service
2780 Via Orange Way, Ste B
Spring Valley, CA 91978
Service that sells secular children's books by direct mail.

The Christian Herald Family Bookshelf
Christian Herald Association
40 Overlook Dr.
Chappaqua, NY 10514
Ed: Mary Risley
914-769-9000

Evangelical Book Club
Div. of Mott Media Inc.
1000 E. Huron St.
Milford, MI 48381
Edit Dir: Sharon Peterson

Guideposts Books
Div. of Guideposts Associates Inc.
16 E. 34th St.
New York, NY 10016
212-251-8100

Jewish Book Club
Box 941
Northvale, NJ 07647
Ed-in-Chief: Arthur Kurzweil
201-767-4093

Jewish Publication Society
1930 Chestnut St.
Philadelphia, PA 19103
Ed-in-chief: Ellen Frankel
215-564-5925

Word Book Club
Word Direct Marketing Services Inc.
Div of ABC/Capital Cities Publishing
5521 N. O'Connor Blvd, Ste 1000
Irving, TX 75039
214-556-1900

Mystery, Suspense, Crime—Genre References

Mystery Writers of America
Priscilla Ridgway, Executive Dir.
17 E. 47th St., 6th Fl
New York, NY 10017

The professional organization of mystery writers.

Membership classes:
Active members - professional writers in the mystery field, meaning that their work has been both published and paid for. (They do not recognize self-published authors in this category.)
Associate members - those who are active in the mystery or crime-writing field in a capacity other than creative writing.
Affiliate members - those who are interested but not active in the mystery or crime-writing field.
Other classes include corresponding, life, honorary, and active elders.

Dues: $65 per year

Membership includes a newsletter, *The Third Degree*, and inclusion in a regional chapter. MWA also has extensive listings available to its members for the cost of postage and photocopying. Lists include bookstores, dealers, libraries, reviewers and wholesalers, all interested in the mystery field, as well as many how-to's on writing and technical advice on criminology.

Awards:

MWA presents the Edgar Allen Poe awards every year in several categories. This is the most prestigious award in the mystery field.

Sisters in Crime
M. Beth Wasson, Executive Secretary
PO Box 442124
Lawrence, KS 66044

Membership dues: $25 per year

Sisters in Crime's purpose is "to combat discrimination against women in the mystery field, educate publishers and the general public as to the inequalities in the treatment of female authors, and raise the level of awareness of their contribution to the field." Despite the feminist slant, they welcome male members, too, and provide excellent marketing and promotion tips for all writers.

Regional and local chapters hold regular meetings and the quarterly newsletter reaches all members. First conference was held August, 1995.

Publications include *Shameless Promotion for Brazen Hussies*, a guide full of promotion ideas, and *So You're Going to do An Author Signing,* which is written both for authors and booksellers who want to plan a successful signing.

Promotional events include booths at the ALA conventions each year, where SinC authors staff the booth and hand out copies of the organization's listing of member *Books in Print.*

Private Eye Writers of America
Martha Dickerson, Membership Sec.
407 W. Third St.
Moorestown, NJ 08057

PWA defines a private investigator as anyone outside government service who does investigative work and is paid for his or her services. This can include detectives, lawyers, medical examiners, and others. If your sleuth fits into this category, PWA welcomes you. Publishes newsletter, "Reflections in a Private Eye"

First conference, EyeCon, was held in 1995. Will probably become a bi-annual event.

Awards:
PWA presents the Shamus Awards in several categories.

International Association of Crime Writers
JAF Box 1500
New York, NY 10116

IACW is an organization of professional writers whose primary goal is to promote communication among writers of all nationalities and to promote crime-writing as an influential and significant art form. They promote the translation of crime writing into other languages and speak with a strong voice to defend authors against censorship and other forms of tyranny. They have branches and members throughout the world.

Membership dues: $50 per year

Membership is open to authors, screenwriters, editors, critics, agents and booksellers.

Other Resources:

There are numerous mystery bookstores nationwide, as well as reviewers who specialize in the genre and libraries with large mystery collections. The listings available through Mystery Writers of America seem to be the most complete on these.

Conferences:

There are nearly a dozen regular mystery conferences held in various places throughout the year. Once you become involed in the genre you'll learn of them. Here are some of the main ones:

Bouchercon (the big one) is held annually in October. It moves to a different location each year. In 1996 it will be in St. Paul, MN; in 1997 it goes to Monterey, CA. It is by far the largest convention, attracting over 2,000 participants each year. Announcements are made in nearly all mystery publications and organization newsletters, to learn where it will be held and find addresses for subsequent years. Attendees of Bouchercon vote on and present the Anthony Awards in honor of Anthony Boucher (rhymes with voucher).

Left Coast Crime, held in February/March, began on the west coast and has traveled around the western states, as far east as Boulder, Colorado in 1996. The 1997 conference will be held in Seattle. Again, check mystery publications to find out location and registration information. Attendees present the Lefty Award for funniest crime novel.

Malice Domestic, P.O. Box 31137, Bethesda, MD 20824-1137. This popular conference celebrates the sub-genre known as the "cozy," and is held in April. Registration fills up each year, so you have to get in early.

Mystery Magazines:

Mystery Scene
Joe Gorman, Editor
PO Box 669
Cedar Rapids, IA 52406-0669
Carries Market News, Regional News, Interviews, Feature articles
by published authors, New Books News, and Reviews

The Mystery Review
Barbara Davey, Editor
PO Box 233
Colborne, ONT K0K 1S0 Canada
Carries Book Reviews, New Releases, Author Interviews, Over
There, a column about British books, Book Shop Beat, featuring a
mystery bookstore, Merchant's Mall and more.

New Mystery Magazine
175 Fifth Ave, Ste 2001
New York, NY 10010
Features Reviews of books, audio and films, short stories.

Book Clubs:

Detective Book Club
Div. of Walter J. Black Inc.
20 W. Vanderventer Ave.
Port Washington, NY 11050
Ed-in-chief: Theodore M. Black Sr.

Mystery Guild
401 Franklin Ave.
Garden City, NY 11530-5945
Ed: Mary Ann Eckels
516-873-4561

Mysterious Book Club
Book of the Month Club Inc.
Time & Life Bldg.
1271 Avenue of the Americas
New York, NY 10020
Ed: Bonnie Thone Boylan
212-522-4200

Internet Sites:

Mysteries From the Yard
Keyword: **Cyber Sleuth** on America Online, or go to
Newstand and choose Mystery Magazines
Features What's New in Mysteries, Meet the Authors, Spy Message
Board, Reference, Bookstore, Children's Mysteries, author chats, A
Guide to Series Mysteries of the Past 25 Years.

Authors can get free listings in the Guide to Series Mysteries and
in the Meet the Authors section. E-mail MsTeries@aol.com to learn
more.

Murder Online
Features publisher and author homepages with full-color book cov-
ers and book excerpts. E-mail Compuserve: 76124.627; America
Online: Byteocrime to learn more.

The Mystery Zone
http://www/mindspring.com/walter/mystzone.html
MWA member Walter Sorrells has created the first internet mystery
magazine. The Mystery Zone features author interviews, cover art,
and many links to other mystery related areas.

DorothyL

Named for Dorothy L. Sayers, this is one of the liveliest discussion groups on the internet. Has over 2,000 members, features a daily e-mail digest, a compilation of messages of interest to mystery readers.

To join, send an e-mail message to: listserv@kentvm.kent.edu

The body of the message should read: sub dorothyl your name. Don't add anything else to the body of the message but your first and last name. You'll receive a welcome e-mail with further instructions on using DorothyL.

Romance—Genre References

Romance Writers of America
13700 Veterans Memorial #315
Houston, TX 77014-1023

A very pro-writer organization. RWA is dedicated to promoting excellence in romantic fiction. General membership is open to all writers actively pursuing a career in romantic fiction. Associate membership is open to all editors, agents, booksellers, and other industry professionals. Nearly 8,000 members worldwide and 140 chapters across the U.S., Canada and Australia.

Annual dues are $60, plus $10 processing fee for new members.

Membership includes:
Romance Writers Report, the official RWA magazine, containing education and technical articles, how-to advice from leading authors, marketplace information, contests and conferences lists (there are many), and "Bookshelf" listings of members books. The magazine also accepts display and classified ads.

A National Conference each year provides writing workshops, published authors workshops, editor/agent appointments, special forums with authors, experts, etc., networking opportunities, Readers for Life Literacy reception, bookseller/librarian reception, publishers summit, and awards ceremony.

There are local and regional chapters of RWA throughout the U.S. and Canada.

Awards:

The RITA Award, the highest award of excellence in the romance genre.

Golden Heart Awards acknowledging promising unpublished authors.

Industry Award to a leader in the romance field.

Janet Dailey Award, presented to a book that deals with a social issue.

Bookseller of the Year

Librarian of the Year

Favorite Book of the Year

ARTemis Award for the year's best cover art

Lifetime Achievement Award

National and Regional Service Awards

The Published Authors Network (PAN) also acts as an advocacy group for published authors and works to increase romance's visibility with librarians and booksellers.

Rose Petals and Pearls
115 Eastmont Drive
Jackson, TN 38301

A non-profit organization dedicated to the preservation of the romance genre. Publishes monthly newsletter (see info below) and sponsors an annual romance author cruise. Sponsors humanitarian projects and performs community services for women, as well as sponsoring literacy programs. Not affiliated with RWA.

Annual dues: $20

Review sources:

Romantic Times
Kathryn Falk, Publisher
163 Joralemon St.
Brooklyn Heights, NY 11201
Features author profiles, news and reviews, letters from authors and from readers, publisher previews, classified and display advertising. They also sponsor such fun events as cruises and parties.

Heart to Heart
Romance at B. Dalton
Division of Barnes & Noble Inc.
122 Fifth Ave.
New York, NY 10011
Reviews and checklists of titles stocked in B. Dalton bookstores. If your books are in B. Dalton stores, send publicity info to this publication.

Gothic Journal
19210 Forest Road N.
Forest Lake, MN 55025-9766
Devoted exclusively to Romantic Suspense, Romantic Mystery, Gothic Romance, Supernatural Romance, Woman-in-Jeopardy Romance (classic and contemporary). Contains reviews, author profiles, market news, industry figure profiles, articles for readers and writers, reader comments on current titles, upcoming titles and shopping lists, drawings and floor plans of great gothic novel settings.

Affaire de Coeur
3976 Oak Hill Drive
Oakland, CA 94605-4931
Contains articles about writing romance fiction, publishing news, author bios, and reviews. Circ. 150,000 monthly.

Love Letters
c/o Maudeen Wachsmith
PO Box 756
Gig Harbor, WA 98335
Uses author interviews and reviews.

Manderley
171 D Brush Street
Ukiah, CA 95482
Review magazine and book catalog.

The Regency Plume Newsletter
Marilyn Clay, Editor
711 D. Street NW
Ardmore, OK 73401
Newsletter for Regency devotees, readers, and writers. Includes market news, upcoming titles, book reviews.

Rose Petals and Pearls
Diane Dirk
115 Eastmont Dr.
Jackson, TN 38301
Includes information about events and articles by romance writers.

Science Fiction/Fantasy/Horror—Genre References

Science Fiction & Fantasy Writers of America
Peter Dennis Pautz, Executive Sec.
5 Winding Brook Dr., Ste 1B
Guilderland, NY 12084

Founded in 1965, SFWA now has over 1200 members throughout the world. They support a Grievance Committee, legal counsel, a Speakers' Bureau, and a Circulating Book Plan. There are special interest groups for writers interested in Young Adult fiction, Poetry, Electronic Publication, and Comics. Various committees monitor contracts and royalty statements, maintain contact with other writer's organizations, set standards for author/agent relations, and help members deal with the strange world of science fiction conventions.

Publishes newsletter, *The SFWA Bulletin*, and the *SFWA Forum* for its active, associate and estate members.

Presents the Nebula® Awards for the SF or Fantasy best short story, novelette, novella, and novel of the year.

Membership is divided into several classes: Active, having professional publication of three short stories or one full-length fiction book in the sci-fi or fantasy genre; Author's Estate's (same as active); Associate, for beginning writers who have at least one professional publication but are not yet eligible for active status; Affiliated members, those associated with the genre, such as agents, editors, reviewers, artists, and publishers; Institutional, for organizations with legitimate interest in sci-fi and fantasy.
[Ed. note: This does not sound like they would recognize self-published authors in the active category.]

Other resources:
Science Fiction Chronicle
PO Box 2730
Brooklyn, NY 11202-0056
Monthly magazine for science fiction, fantasy and horror writers.

The Small Press Genre Association
Cathy Hicks, Secretary
16822 W. Savage Rd.
Marana, AZ 85653

The SPGA exists to promote excellence in writing, illustration, calligraphy, editing and publication of material related to the literary genre of fantasy, sword & sorcery, horror, western, mystery, weird, or science fiction in publications with limited distribution, including small press comics in the same genre. Membership is open to any writer, poet, artist, editor, publisher or calligrapher who participates in these genre.

Members receive the quarterly publication, *The Genre Writer's News* which includes articles on writing and artistry, market news, reviews of small press productions, news about the membership, fiction, poetry and artwork all from SPGA members. In alternate months, members receive The Market News Supplement.

Dues are $25 in the U.S., $30 elsewhere.
(Note: We are including this organization in this section because in the sample we reviewed of their materials, we found almost nothing of western or mystery and felt it belong more correctly under the heading of Sci-Fi/Fantasy/Horror. Authors and publishers of other genre are certainly welcome to request a sample copy of the publication before making a decision as to its appropriateness for your use.)

Book Clubs:
The Science Fiction Book Club
1540 Broadway, 23rd Fl.
New York, NY 10036
Ed-in-Chief: Ellen Asher
212-782-7278

Conferences:

There are so many conferences and fan conventions in the Sci-Fi/Fantasy genre each year that it is impossible to list them here. Check fanzines and newsletters to learn of more.

Or subscribe to Science Fiction Convention Register, PO Box 3343, Fairfax, VA 22038, 703-273-3297. This register lists over 500 conventions in the genre, and is published three times per year.

Magazines—Review Sources

Science Fiction Chronicle
PO Box 022730
Brooklyn, NY 11202-0056
To get a book reviewed, send galleys to Don D'Ammassa, Book Review Editor, 323 Dodge St, E. Providence, RI 02914. Also send final copies of all books to both addresses.

Science Fiction Eye
c/o Eyeball Books
PO Box 18539
Asheville, NC 28814
Carries a mix of reviews, commentary, criticism, debate, interviews and essays.

Western—Genre Resources

Western Writers of America
Candy Moulton, Membership Chairman
Box 29 Star Route
Encampment, WY 82325

Formed in the early 1950s, Western Writers of America now has a membership of about 500, representing 40 states and several foreign countries. Membership includes a subscription to the organization magazine, *Roundup*.

Membership categories: Active members are working professional writers with book and magazine publishing credits. Associate members may be newcomers to the western field, editors, publishers, booksellers, agents, artists, and writers still reaching for the goal of professional status.

Dues are $60 per year for either category.

Awards:
Spur Awards are presented in several categories, including best western books of fiction, nonfiction, juvenile books, and TV and film scripts.

Conferences:
An annual conference is held in a different western city each year, affording opportunities for writers to meet other writers, editors, publishers and book people in general. The conference also features workshops, panels, films and other events.

Other Organizations of Interest

American Book Producers Association
160 5th Ave., Suite 604
New York, NY 10010-7000

American Society of Journalists and Authors
1501 Broadway, Suite 302
New York, NY 10036

Association of Desk-Top Publishers
4677 30th St, #800
San Diego, CA 92116-3245

The Authors Guild
330 W. 42nd St.
New York, NY 10036

The Book Industry Study Group
Bill Raggio
160 Fifth Ave.
New York, NY 10010
(conducts surveys on book sales, listing breakdowns in nearly every
conceivable category)

Council of Authors & Journalists
c/o Uncle Remus Regional Library System
1131 East Ave.
Madison, GA 30650

Council of Literary Magazines & Presses
154 Christopher St, Ste 3C
New York, NY 10014

National Writers Club
1450 S. Havana, Ste 424
Aurora, CO 80012

Poetry Society of America
15 Grammercy Park
New York, NY 10012

Poets & Writers
72 Spring St.
New York, NY 10012

Writers Connection
1061 Saratoga-Sunnyvale Rd., Ste 180
Cupertino, CA 95014

Writers Guild of America (East)
555 W. 57th St.
New York, NY 10019

Writers Guild of America (West)
8955 Beverly Blvd.
West Hollywood, CA 90048

Also check for local and regional writers organizations in your own area. Networking with writers, booksellers, and librarians in your own city and state can provide many valuable contacts that cannot be reached through a national organization.

Index

F

G

H

I

Order Form

Order additional copies of *Publish Your Own Novel* for your writer friends, for business associates, or for classroom use.

Call 1-800-996-9783 to order by credit card.

Or copy and mail this form to: Columbine Books, P.O. Box 456, Angel Fire, NM 87710

Name _____

Company _____

Address _____

City, ST, Zip _____

Daytime phone _____

_____ copies of *Publish Your Own Novel* at $18.95 each _____

Shipping $3.00 for first book, $1.00 each additional _____

NM residents add $1.15 tax per book _____

Total _____

Payment: ___ Check ___ Mastercard or Visa

Card # _____

Exp Date _____ Signature _____

Or **call 1-800-996-9783** to order now by credit card.
Ask about our quantity discounts on orders of 5 copies or more.